Whither Thou Goest

D0573022

Whither Thou Goest

The Story of an Uprooted Wife

By Eleanor Dienstag

E.P. Dutton & Co., Inc. | New York | 1976

CT
275
D463
A34
1976

Copyright © 1976 by Eleanor Dienstag
All rights reserved. Printed in the U.S.A.
First Edition
10   9   8   7   6   5   4   3   2   1

No part of this publication may be reproduced or transmitted in any form
or by any means, electronic or mechanical, including photocopy, recording,
or any information storage and retrieval system now known or to be invented, without permission in writing from the publisher, except by a reviewer who wishes to quote brief passages in connection with a review
vritten for inclusion in a magazine, newspaper or broadcast.

Published simultaneously in Canada by
Clarke, Irwin & Company Limited, Toronto and Vancouver

ISBN: 0–525–23314–8

Library of Congress Cataloging in Publication Data

Dienstag, Eleanor.
    Whither thou goest.

    1. Dienstag, Eleanor.   I. Title.
CT275.D463A34   1976   973.92'092'4   [B]   75–25751

In memory of Hal Scharlatt
and
for Zena

116376

116376

FOREWORD

This book is an act of sharing. It is a personal book about being uprooted because of a husband's career and about the crises that preceded and succeeded leaving home.

My "home town" happened to be New York City, an island not normally associated with that special state of inner peace that comes from growing up and putting down roots in one place. But this could be the story of a woman from anywhere torn from the life she knew and loved, faced with the real and psychological shocks of relocation. Despite the apparent uniqueness of my move from a big city to a smaller one, I carried with me the anxiety and loneliness, the loss, displaced anger, and sense of helplessness that are the universal baggage of the uprooted wife.

Statistics tell us that 40 percent of the population moves every four years, but in government or in cities dominated by a large university or corporation, the mobility seems even greater. Moving upward and onward has always been an American tradition. Symbiotically attached to that tradition has been "the good wife" who followed her man no matter what he did or where he went. But for those men and women who are grappling with the implications of the feminist revolution, the wife's duty to follow is no longer automatic. The cheerfully loyal, peripatetic spouse is another national ideal whose foundations are crumbling.

The issue of career mobility lies at the heart of the present battle between men and women. (Men following successful career wives is an increasing phenomenon and equally fraught with danger.) It is a raw nerve, universally experienced, regardless of whether one accepts or rejects conventional marriage.

There is no one solution to this problem, nor are there any guidance counselors trained to ease the pain of transition. One can only ask the right questions. Perhaps this book will help others pose to themselves and their partners the right questions at the right time.

"Never confuse movement with action."
—Ernest Hemingway

Fall 1969

CHAPTER I

One October evening, in the fall of 1969, my husband came home from the office, sat down on our recently acquired sofa, and said, his eyes rooted on a design in our Oriental rug, "I'm afraid I've just been offered an extraordinary job in Rochester."

We were seated in the olympic-sized living room of our rent-controlled apartment on West Seventy-ninth Street in Manhattan. We had lived there six of the eleven years of our marriage and regarded it less as a dwelling place than our spiritual home.

To New Yorkers, the quest for that big, rent-controlled-apartment-in-the-sky was what the Holy Grail must have been to the Knights of the Round Table: a moral drama posing as an athletic pursuit. Not only did one have to be physically aggressive, cunning, and obsessed but also, in some inexplicable sense, worthy of the prize: a commitment to the city was being tested. Those who gave up and accepted the suburban commuter compromise were felt, however irrationally, to deserve their fate.

Although we had triumphed, we never ceased to marvel at our good fortune. Our six rooms possessed a dramatic view of the Hudson, high ceilings, inlaid floors, foot-thick walls, gracious moldings, and no roaches. We were a block from Riverside Park, within walking distance of a neighborhood my mother-in-law had pronounced "good shopping," and two mugproof blocks from the Seventh Avenue subway— granted one avoided the temptation of midnight strolls. I had devoted twelve years of my life to making the city work for us and I was very good at that job. A small town demands different survival techniques; a house requires different care; a car takes skill to manage. In such a situation I would be like a dolphin in the desert.

To our friends we were affectionately known as fanatic New Yorkers; to outsiders we were provincial New Yorkers, the kind of people innocent of the amenities of life outside a concrete cage. There is some truth to that point of view. To love New York is probably to be slightly mad. But most passions are an expression of insanity—temporary or not—and I had come by mine honestly.

I was thirty-one years old and had lived in various parts of Manhattan since the age of eight. My husband, Jerry, born and raised in Brooklyn, had forded the East River during law school and never seriously looked back. While I was not technically a native, having been born in Naples, Italy, a rare species of that vanishing breed, the Italian Jew, I felt that oneness with the city that is common to any hometown citizen anywhere. New York was never a vast impersonal labyrinth, but a series of neighborhoods in which I felt comfortable and known. The tailor, pharmacist, and small shopkeepers knew one by name, and so did the butcher and the vegetable man at the supermarket. As a child my city had been a circumscribed neighborhood; as a teen-ager, an exhaustless treasure of museums and shops; as a working woman, a world in which ambition and success were open-ended. Most recently, as a full-time mother and housewife, I had savored the city's endless montage of street life. Contrary to the cliché that New York is best suited to couples without children, I had become increasingly convinced that it was an ideal setting for my carriage-pushing years.

It seemed beyond the range of probability that we would ever discuss leaving. The past year had marked the culmination of my nesting drive, a year almost exclusively devoted to painting, papering, and painstakingly refurbishing our back bedroom to function efficiently with two boys, aged four and six months, in active residence. There was no doubt in my mind that we were settled for good. Forever.

So when my husband came home that evening with the news, it was as though he had said, "You have two months to live." It couldn't be real. It couldn't be happening to me. *Other* women married upwardly mobile executives. *Other* women switched friends and country clubs like furniture in a room. But "they" and "them" had suddenly become me. I felt as though my execution had just been announced.

Of course, I should have seen it coming. There had been signs all around me that I preferred to ignore.

There was the fact that my husband, a financially successful corporate and securities lawyer, was not enjoying his practice and didn't know what to do about it. (Over-thirty-five angst, I said. He'll get over it.) There were those business trips to Phoenix and Cleveland and Rochester, from which he had returned, saying, "You know, it's not so bad out there." (Expense-account traveling, I said. Any place looks good for a day.) There was his increased irritability with the quality of city life. (He's learning to cope with two kids, I said. He'll adjust.)

Besides, everyone complained about New York. It was the great, middle-class indoor sport. John Lindsay fiddled while Rome burned. Problems were out of control. The barbarians were at the gates. Hard-line loyalists bitched about the ankle-deep dog shit, the fear of assault, rising costs, decaying schools, and diminished civilities. At parties, the horror story of the week was gaily passed around with pâté from Bloomingdale's. But let someone's aunt from Chevy Chase express trepidation at visiting the city, and incredulous looks were exchanged. People are fiercely loyal to the places they love and feel that whatever they have to put up with is worth it.

How was I to know that in my husband the disaffection had gone deeper? Or that his less-flippantly delivered remark on the subject of living in New York, "It's a nice place to live, but I wouldn't want to work there," reflected the subtle tension that different routines can create between a husband and wife. Jerry felt battered by the nervous energy of the city. I felt buoyed by it. He perceived himself the front-line soldier; his wife, a privileged visitor to the battlefield. Since the birth of our first child, the stresses upon our lives had emanated from dissimilar sources. But since I was not a suburban wife, since we both dealt with the problems and pleasures of city living, I was hardly aware of our increasingly divergent perspectives.

What made my husband's announcement even more startling was that he had not been looking for a job. Perhaps, like a married man on the prowl, his availability was unmistakable. But to me, the offer had come without warning.

The *deus ex machina* was a Rochester lawyer, Harold Yanowitch, whom Jerry had met and worked with on a small public offering the year before. That morning he had asked Jerry by phone to join a modular-housing company, Stirling Homex.

As far as my husband knew, Yanowitch possessed a rare gift that cannot be taught in law school—the ability to snare and keep rich clients. In his fifties, with five children and a five-acre estate to support, it was surprising to hear he had given up his lucrative private practice to join a fledgling company as executive vice-president and general counsel. But he was now putting together a crack legal team and wanted Jerry as his securities and corporate expert. No salary had been mentioned.

Over the years, especially since Jerry had begun traveling around the country in connection with stock deals and acquisitions, he had received innumerable offers to leave New York. He had been flattered but uninterested. This time it was different. He assured me he had played it cool, but I could tell from the barely suppressed excitement in his voice that the proposal was shimmering in his imagination. He had agreed to fly to Rochester to see what it was all about.

I met my husband in the summer of 1956. I was eighteen years old, between my freshman and sophomore years at

Smith, on my way to France, third class, aboard the luxury liner *Liberté*. Ostensibly, I was to visit Paris with friends and pursue my mastery of French at the University of Grenoble, but I viewed the adventure as my freedom summer, my great escape.

I was a serious young woman formed by literature not by life—I knew more about Madame Bovary than about my mother—and thought of my trip not as a 1950s version of the grand tour, but as a Jamesian quest for identity.

I was, then, an easy mark for any man who took me seriously, who was as charmed by my brain as my body. Unexpectedly, and despite my fantasies of European lovers, Jerry Dienstag was that man. He was also on board ship, a twenty-two-year-old Columbia law student, and not at all what I had in mind. In his drip-dry shirts and khakis, this nice Jewish boy from Brooklyn was about as exotic as a breakfast of Wheaties.

Whether we seduced each other in Paris or were seduced by the romantic idea of falling in love in Paris doesn't really matter. What matters is that he pursued me with irresistible single-mindedness, and that we followed the scenario prescribed for sexually aroused Americans of our generation. Two summers later, after Jerry's graduation from law school, I transferred to Barnard and we got married. I was a June bride.

We shared a love of books and movies. He was a fine dancer and once-serious musician, and I was a sucker for any man with a sense of rhythm. He was a nice amalgam of the tender and the tough, and he possessed a host of qualities I thought I lacked: a quick wit, a salesman's gift for storytelling and for sizing up people, an extroverted, articulate personality overflowing with charm. I was the silent brooder, incapable of small talk. My thoughts were often illogical and poorly expressed, except on paper. I was always asking what-is-the-purpose-of-life questions. Jerry was more interested in the practical necessities. I was the romantic; he was the realist. But above all, Jerry brought out the best in me. He was my number-one fan. In his company I was funnier, gayer, sharper. In his presence I was what I could become. His confidence energized me.

To say we had never thought about the realities of marriage is to begin to approach the truth. For two years we had plotted, schemed, overcome my parents' violent disapproval, for what? For the privilege of legitimizing our sex lives. I had not the slightest interest in becoming a housewife or, god forbid, a mother. All I wanted was a friend, a permanent Saturday night date who would be warm and supportive while I figured out in which direction lay my life's work. What I got, instead, was a husband, a perfectly normal male who, without meditating on the particulars, expected a wife.

It is a cliché to say that you know nothing about a person until you have lived with him. But it will always strike me as peculiar that a woman who believed herself so perceptive knew so little about the man she married. He might as well have been a stranger I had picked up off the street.

Jerry was conventional, but after my years of adolescent rebellion, of floating around New York in purple stockings and Bohemian uniforms, there was something solid and comforting about his indifference to poetic masks. He was a grownup, and that, after all, was my ambition: to marry a real man.

Like most of my friends who stampeded directly from college to marriage, I had never cared for a home, cooked a meal, balanced a checkbook, or in any way experienced the normal responsibilities of an adult. Neither had Jerry for that matter. So it came as something of a shock to discover, after our Bermuda honeymoon, that though Jerry and I were both working full time, I was expected at night to shop for dinner, cook, and clean up while Jerry settled himself on our easy chair with *The New York Post.*

Jerry thought me crazy for complaining. Men weren't supposed to help out. Everyone knew and accepted that. What was wrong with me? Why had I married in the first place? In 1958, there was only one answer: I was selfish, immature, and lazy. Although, in our first disputes, I countered that such epithets more accurately fit Jerry, part of me accepted his judgment.

We were both working, so the argument went, but the stakes were different. For me it was only a summer job, a glamorous sinecure as secretary to the Ethiopian ambassador to the United Nations. My work mainly consisted of writing invitations to parties in honor of His Excellency Haile Selassie's birthday, attending the parties, and avoiding the lecherous advances of the ambassador's staff. It contrasted painfully with Jerry's forty-five-dollar-a-week errand-boy chores for a large law firm he despised. Jerry had been indifferent to law school and was now paying for it. Although I was convinced he had whatever it took to become successful, he was riddled with self-doubt. The lower depths of the legal profession terrified him. Suddenly, my self-confident suitor, that life of the party, was transformed into a depressed, silent husband. He was haunted by the failures he observed in court. Would he wind up haggling over five hundred-dollar insurance and negligence cases, angry, bored, cynical, hustling for clients, barely making ends meet? It was a bad beginning, exacerbated by my amateur standing in the real world. I had one more year of college in which to fool around. My nine-to-five job was fun and games, so how could I expect my husband to equate his daily grind with mine? Of course he supported ambitions in a woman that went beyond perfecting her pot roast. But they were not to interfere with traditional duties. Especially since Jerry was the sort of man who could die of starvation next to a full refrigerator. My luck. I had married a Jewish prince.

A Jewish prince knows where to buy the best cheesecake, but lacks the manual dexterity to cut it. A Jewish prince likes tea with a slice of fresh lemon, but can never find the lemon. A Jewish prince sees his home not as an expression of himself, but as a refuge from the world, a place to sleep and eat, where no requests are made and the daily fabric of domestic life is invisibly mended. A Jewish prince is a boarder in his own house who, when asked to contribute more than the rent, defends his passivity by shrieking, "You don't know what it's like out there!"

Indeed, I did not. For the first year of our marriage I

romped through my college courses and played house. But after graduation I discovered that the waves did not part for a woman with a B.A. in history.

During my last year of school I became deeply interested in writing, but unsure about breaking into print—or not—I chose what was then a respectable career for a woman with literary sensibilities—book publishing.

In those days, few outsiders took the book business very seriously. It was perceived—not altogether incorrectly—as a refuge for unacademic English majors, a safe harbor for failed writers, dreamy dilettantes, young men and women with romantic notions about literature and an Ivy-League contempt for money.

I was no exception. To me books were holy. As to how they were selected, edited, printed, designed, or distributed, I knew nothing, except what I had picked up from reading the lofty letters of Maxwell Perkins to his star authors. It was as if I had read Churchill's speeches to find out what politics was all about. Being an editor, I thought, was like dining with the Gods.

My first job brought me down to earth fast. I became an editorial secretary at Prentice-Hall, a publishing factory with no literary pretensions. Its textbook division made the money; its trade department (general fiction and nonfiction), where I resided, lost it. Within weeks of my arrival I was looking for ways to get out.

After a few months I got lucky and landed a coveted job as a manuscript reader in the trade department of Harper & Brothers, now Harper & Row. It was the lowest rung on the editorial ladder, but I was sprung from the well-known secretarial trap and on my way.

Harper & Brothers enjoyed an exalted reputation. It was the Harvard of its field—one of the oldest, one of the best, respectable without being stodgy, the publishing arm of the eastern establishment. Its roster of authors included Harry Hopkins, Robert Sherwood, Dean Acheson, Walter Rostow, George Kennan, Adlai Stevenson, the Kennedy clan, Eleanor Roosevelt, Harrison Salisbury, and a relatively obscure but promising Harvard professor by the name of Henry Kissinger whose manuscript for *The Necessity for Choice* was the subject of my first reader's report.

The first week of my job I became ill with the flu. When I returned to the office, a male colleague informed me that our immediate boss had inquired whether I was pregnant. I was astonished but thought little more about the incident until, gradually, I understood what it meant.

The assumption, rampant in book publishing, was that married women were not serious about a career, were marking time before motherhood. This discriminatory mentality became a self-fulfilling prophecy. Women were rarely top-level editors. The exceptions, largely relegated to such marginal fields as poetry, cookbooks, suspense, and juveniles, were spinsters, widows, or middle-aged brides, reliably barren.

For several years I worked very hard, assuming that my obvious talent for editing would be rewarded, that my uniqueness would be recognized. Nothing in my background had prepared me for failure, and as the elder of two daughters, nothing had prepared me for second-class citizenship. I considered myself bright and dedicated and had already scored a coup with the publication of my first article in *Harper's Magazine.* At sales meetings and editorial conferences I was treated with respect by the higher-ups and interpreted their deference as a sign of my growing stature within the Harper family. I couldn't have been more mistaken. When a recession finally hit the industry in 1961 I, along with a number of other women, was fired.

The shock and humiliation of being fired could not have come at a worse moment because my marriage, after three years, was falling apart. The double standard I had encountered at work was nothing compared to the double standard I was discovering in my husband. Once he had successfully carried off his child bride, it occurred to him, with growing uneasiness, that he was bound and tied to one woman for life. With marriage came the loss of freedom, the obligation to come home every night to the emotional demands of an insecure woman who expected, like most women of her generation, fidelity.

Trapped, Jerry sang me the litany of his generation: men could sleep around, but women, since they became "emotionally involved," could not. Whether or not he made good on this theory was hardly the issue. Threatened, I turned into a jealous wife. In Jerry's view, a little dishonesty between man and wife made for a lasting marriage—assuming the wife was faithful. Lechery was a male prerogative.

Jerry, I believe, had little notion of the havoc his theories were creating. He thought of himself as a good husband, not excessively cruel or flirtatious, just a normal guy having normal second thoughts about the contradictions of marriage. He was also going through the worst years of his professional life, earning very little money and moving in and out of a series of jobs with no future and no promise of success. As his self-confidence ebbed, my indifference grew. No doubt he was expressing exaggerated male fantasies of sexual power as a way of compensating for his temporary but real impotence as a lawyer. I should have understood that need to substitute sexual success for career success since I myself felt thwarted at Harper's, stuck in a slot and categorized by gender.

Like many women denied access to real power, I began to daydream about the only power left me: seducing successful men. I had last experienced such fantasies as an adolescent, hopelessly in love with movie stars. But as a grown woman I began to wonder if they were not possible, if I had not sold myself in marriage too cheaply.

Thus goaded, in an attempt to gain some of the rewards neither my marriage nor my job was providing, I embarked on a brief, not unpleasant, retaliatory affair. When I lost my job, illusions about my strength, invincibility, and value crumbled like the Maginot line. I was a failure as a wife, a married man's diffident mistress, a writer with one article to her credit that had taken two years to write and a career washout.

In this depressed state of mind, I took what I felt was drastic action: I went to a psychiatrist.

When I began seeing a psychiatrist three times a week, I had no desire to save the marriage; I only wanted to save myself. It had never been a marriage, just a series of constricting rituals that both of us had raged at, for different reasons, from the start. But the doctor urged me to make no radical decisions while I was in such a state of confusion, and I agreed.

Jerry's reasons for hanging in were, as far as I could tell, utterly conventional. In those days there was a terrible stigma attached to divorce. Like suicide, there was never a good enough reason. It wasn't done.

Neither of us had the courage to face what we assumed were the consequences of such an action. Jerry had convinced me that to men a divorcee was an object of pity and sexual availability. He painted a picture of unremitting loneliness and I bought it. And for all of Jerry's braggadocio, he was not a swinger. He wanted to be free, not alone. He desired the convenience of marriage, not a wife. We were like two hollow walls, unable to stand apart, leaning upon one another for support.

The psychiatrist led me to understand that the first step toward confronting my problems was to end the affair. I agreed but abandoned my fantasies of male conquest with a mixture of relief and dread. Although the affair had brought me no happiness, it had enabled me to cope with the bleakness of my real life. How would I function without the artificial crutch of romance?

Of all my problems, a job seemed the easiest to deal with. I had many friends in the book business who encouraged me to hold out for a position equal to the one I had lost. Although I was out of work for six months, I eventually landed an identical job at Random House.

My social life bloomed, but it became clear that Random House was even more of a dead end than Harper's. I felt invisible. So did my office mate who, upon giving notice, quipped, "It took me six weeks to find anyone to quit to!"

I stuck it out for a year and resigned at the first opportunity to join a struggling, new magazine of political satire, *Mono-*

cle, where at last, talent and hard work were the only level-
ers.

We worked out of the roach-infested, ground-floor apartment of our editor, Victor Navasky, and it proved to be the
happiest job experience of my life. Not only did I love my
colleagues, but I also got the chance to write articles, edit,
learn layout and how to put a magazine together.

Between 1961 and 1964, when I was not contributing to
the mechanics of publishing and editing, I turned out a series
of pieces for *Monocle,* ranging from "Happy Rockefeller's
Secret Diary" to a straight investigation of seamy publishing
practices at Macmillan. In my spare time I continued to write
short stories and literary essays that no one published, but my
work for *Monocle* caught the attention of various editors.
With Victor Navasky as my unflagging promoter, book review and article assignments from *The New Republic, The
New York Herald Tribune,* and even *The New York Times*
began to trickle in.

Not only was my career opening up new avenues of pleasure, but since 1961 Jerry's career had taken an unexpected
leap forward although, despite these successes, our marriage
was still in a holding pattern. Through a series of chance
encounters, he stumbled into the securities field, which was
then experiencing its greatest boom since the depression. His
salary tripled, and he was initiated into the heady atmosphere of big money by two attorneys in their thirties who
were bringing in public-minded clients faster than they
could turn out registration statements.

To an ambitious young man who had been performing
routine duties in a moldering law firm, the daily excitement
of securities work was intoxicating. The pressure of SEC
deadlines, the ability to extract facts from duplicitous sources
(often one's client), the talent to create a document of readable prose, the stamina to nurse a registration through the
printer, staying with it day and night and then dashing down
to Washington with the freshly minted document in hand,
created a cult of fast-talking, fast-living men.

Many lawyers couldn't take the stress and retreated, happily, to the quiet dignity of trusts and wills. For others, it became a passion. The stakes were enormous. Lawyers were like casino owners raking in the cash from both ends. Not only were fees high, but also attorneys were often given a piece of the deal. In a rising market, thousands of shares of cheap stock increased in value with dizzying swiftness. While once young men had to struggle for years to build a practice, now many became millionaires overnight.

Jerry had been underpaid and underworked too long not to enjoy the salary, the frenzied pace, and the power. Being the lynch-pin in million-dollar deals, the key man without whom this extravagant shuffling of money could not take place, was pure pleasure. But like all men on the rise, he found himself thrust into a world of charming, ruthless careerists whose values were both attractive and absurd. They dreamt of Connecticut estates, a Rolls-Royce in the garage, a closetful of handmade suits, and being greeted on a first-name basis by the maître d' at four-star restaurants. I knew their type well. Publishing was full of them. New York thrived on their snobberies. Jerry was incapable of identifying with their driven souls. He enjoyed money but would not toady to fools to get it. He enjoyed hard work but not exclusively. He had a taste for elegant restaurants and suits, but only as enjoyment. Slowly, we began to pull together as husband and wife. We were united in our sardonic view of fame and fortune, although a part of us hoped there was a virtuous and sensible way to the top.

The market crash of 1962 ended the first mad season. *Monocle,* which was about to raise its working capital by going public, withdrew its offering. My salary temporarily ceased. Jerry's law firm, which had been taking on new lawyers and upgrading its offices, dissolved almost overnight. But we took these reverses with equanimity since we had begun to realize that we had a future together. I kept my faith in *Monocle*'s ability to survive and was proved correct. Jerry reentered the conventional practice of the law, chastened by the experience and more self-confident. We were grateful we still lived in our three-room hovel and had no children.

Indeed, the only mistake we didn't make as a young married couple was to imagine our problems could be solved by having a child. The prospect of motherhood terrified me. It was like a black cloud hovering at the edge of my vision. When I first began to have good feelings about being a mother, I wondered if the crisis in our marriage had not passed. It was as though a maze had resolved itself into a series of straight corridors, all leading out. After all those years of inchoate emotion, of feeling myself a victim, I was in control—a grownup. I was ready to take responsibility for myself. I felt free.

The process that renewed us was imperceptible. Certainly we no longer expected the marriage to compensate for our external setbacks. And there were fewer of them. Others saw us as a bright, up and coming couple—not as a pair of life's losers—and so did we. Our friends and work were more stimulating. We were not the kind of people who analyzed how and why we had changed, admitting past faults and setting forth new guidelines. We still communicated our feelings through an elaborate code of humor and gestures, but the renewed signs of affection were unmistakable.

I remember the day I understood a significant inner change had taken place. Lying on the living room couch, eyes closed, I saw myself in an enormous, empty room with dozens of windows, their shades fully drawn. Each shade was an aspect of my personality. Each was clearly marked—Wife, Writer, Child, and so forth. Suddenly I realized each shade could be raised and lowered separately. A flick of my wrist would not set off an uncontrollable chain reaction. Instead, I could illuminate the room only when I was prepared to face the light. Yes, I could be a wife without becoming a 1950s version of The Wife. I could become a mother without denying myself a career. I could enjoy my sexual powers without feeling used.

I was ready, too, to deal with this complicated stranger I had married. He used humor to keep pain and humiliation at a distance. His extrovert's mask covered a shyness and insecurity equal to my own. His fear of commitment and emotional intimacy had been fashioned into a sexual weapon. Jerry was no longer a stranger, but a fascinating and familiar puzzle I had grown rather fond of putting together.

By our fifth year of marriage, when so many of our friends' ill-conceived unions to college sweethearts were dissolving, we knew we had come through. We had fallen in love again. There was no climactic reunion. Instead, we began making plans for the future.

Not everything was resolved between us or within us. I had not come to grips with what was muddling my brain every time I sat down to write, especially when I tackled the higher calling of fiction, but still I was turning out good work for *Monocle*, as well as many of the best publications in the country. Jerry had still not found his niche as a lawyer, but was temporarily content in a small firm that allowed him to build his own practice. We admired each other more and expected less. We accepted each other's strengths and weaknesses with candor. After all, who is perfect?

Feeling flush, Jerry and I treated ourselves to our first grand vacation. In the summer of 1963 we flew to Billings, Montana, rented a car, toured the national parks, drove to Oregon and then all the way down the Pacific Coast to San Diego. The three-week trip momentarily stunned us out of our New York provincialism. It was gorgeous "out there." Returning to New York, we began to crave light, space, and a view. Jerry launched a frenzied search for a new apartment. I endured pinches and gropings from doormen and superintendents in return for doors being unlocked to unlisted gems. Within six months we had found the apartment on Seventy-ninth Street where, it was clear, we would put down permanent roots and raise a family.

By the summer of 1964 *Monocle* was running out of money. The assassination of John Kennedy had diminished America's appetite for satire. But my free-lance career was growing and it seemed reasonable to assume that if I cul-

116376

tivated my publishing friends and conspired with an agent,
I would have more work than I could handle. It was the
solution to the career versus motherhood problem. I would
write at home, which would leave me as much time as I
needed to remain a good wife and mother.

My first son, Joshua, was born in the spring of 1965. By
summer I had settled into an ideal routine of writing when
he slept, long strolls with the carriage, and leisurely times at
home with Joshua at my breast. I was enthralled with my
child. How could I have ever contemplated not having a
baby? He aroused whole new feelings: joy, protectiveness,
responsibility, tremulous fears of loss and tragedy that made
me wonder if, before his birth, I had only been half alive. It
brought me closer to my parents. By doing something *I*
wanted, I had at last done something *they* wanted. I was the
first of my friends to have a baby. He was my parents' first
grandchild. Everyone was fascinated by *what it was really
like.* Well, I freely admitted, it was glorious.

Two years later I eagerly became pregnant again, but it
was not the instant replay I had expected. My first pregnancy
had been an unbroken physical high, but now I was plagued
with a host of minor discomforts that culminated in a sev-
enth-month miscarriage. I was twenty pounds overweight,
had resumed smoking after two years of abstinence, and was
depressed. Joshua was demanding more of my time, and
although a two-day-a-week baby-sitter freed me to write in
a neighbor's apartment across the street, my work was not
going well. I was in the midst of a crisis of direction as a writer
that eventually became total paralysis.

My free-lance career had largely been unplanned and it
had been my misfortune, in a sense, to start at the top. Without the will to seek out work, my free-lance career dribbled
away. So I concentrated on fiction but not a line of it ever
sold.

Gradually, and without ever admitting it, I gave up. By the
time my second son was born in 1969 I had ceased writing
altogether. To my friends, I was just taking time out to have

children. Inwardly I felt myself a failed writer, but perhaps because I was older, because I had a life outside writing and recognized there were other interesting work options in New York, I was not despondent. In fact I was laying plans for my future. I had already mentioned to Jerry the possibility of returning to editing on a part-time basis, the following fall. Not in book but magazine publishing. I was ready to get out of the house and back in the adult world again.

While I had been adjusting to motherhood, Jerry's career had again taken a new direction. In 1966 he decided to make the big move and set up his own practice. Hedging his bet, he rented a room in a legal suite of offices at 63 Wall Street. The idea was to pay his rent by taking the work overflow of two corporate lawyers in adjoining rooms. That arrangement lasted barely six months. The stock market was once more risking capital in new issues and Jerry's expertise in registration work again became invaluable. The lawyers with whom he was loosely associated were inundated with public-minded companies. Slowly but inevitably Jerry began devoting more of his time to these clients. Within a year he formally joined their law firm and the second gold rush was on.

Jerry vowed the mistakes of the past would not be repeated. This time around he would not allow the firm to only concentrate on sending companies public. Instead, they would build a corporate practice out of their new clients. But as a junior partner, drawing a salary and a portion of the profits, he was not in a position to call the shots. The senior partners had already made their first million and forgotten the crash of 1962. They scoffed at Jerry's conservatism. Instead of keeping down the overhead, they abandoned the modest offices on Wall Street and made plans to take over the top floor of a new midtown tower on Park Avenue. It was the 1961 folly all over again. Jerry opposed the expansion, especially since, by the middle of 1969, the market was showing familiar signs of slipping. But he was making forty thousand dollars a year, had a wife and two children to support and saw no alternatives. The Wall Street lease expired before the Park Avenue palace was habitable. The firm moved to depressing, temporary quarters in the Commodore Hotel. It was precisely during this interim period, when Jerry's spirits were at their lowest, that Yanowitch placed his call. No wonder it seemed like a godsend.

CHAPTER II

John Brooks, in a series of articles in *The New Yorker*, dubbed the sixties "the go-go years" of the stock market. "In 1968–69," he perceptively noted, "what a promoter needed to launch a new stock, apart from a persuasive tongue and a resourceful accountant, was a 'story'—an easily grasped concept, preferably related to some current national fad or preoccupation, that *sounded* as if it would lead to profits."

In those terms, Stirling Homex was the quintessential go-go stock.

Their "story" was instant housing. The current national obsession, equal to A Cure for Cancer, was A Decent Home for Every American. The federal government, under President Lyndon Johnson, was committed to it. And it sounded as if the techniques of mass production, if applied to housing, would logically lead to profits.

Modular housing was not a new idea but, in America, building a complete home on an assembly line was a new business. It seemed an idea whose time had come. But while big-name companies like ITT-Levitt and National Homes were just launching their modular operations, Stirling Homex was already a proven winner—the leading manufacturer of factory-produced, low-cost housing in the country. With an astonishing 10 percent net-after-tax profit.

Although the company was not yet two years old, and the brainchild of two small-town builders, David and William Stirling, it had already begun the lengthy and complicated process of going public. When Harold Yanowitch called Jerry, Homex's preliminary prospectus was on file with the Securities and Exchange Commission. Jerry requested a copy of the document, confident he could read between the lines as well as any Wall Street expert.

The investment firm underwriting the offering was R. W. Pressprich & Company, a respectable brokerage house whose spectacular performance with Ross Perot's Electronic Data Systems was on everyone's mind. Would Homex become another hot stock like EDS?

A prominent member of Homex's board of directors was Theodore Kheel, a New York labor lawyer who mediated a breakthrough contract between Homex and the United Brotherhood of Carpenters and Joiners. Opposition to modular housing had traditionally come from the unions. But now, in a single stroke, that opposition had been removed. Union members were already working on Homex's assembly line.

So this was not a marginal company, promoted by sleazy hucksters, of which there were so many in the get-rich atmosphere of Wall Street during the late sixties. Jerry was impressed with the facts in the prospectus; nevertheless, between the time he talked with Yanowitch and flew to Rochester, he continued to check the company out.

Everyone from a Lehman Brothers investment banker to a "top man" at First National City Bank gave the company an A-number-one rating. No one voiced the slightest skepticism except my father, and that was more in the form of a joke. As an economist, now the American representative of an Italian real-estate giant, he took one look at Homex's financial statement and said, "It's too good to be true."

But wasn't that precisely why the investment community was drooling with anticipation? Hadn't Homex discovered the trick of cutting costs in a notoriously inefficient industry?

The truth was Jerry needed little convincing. For years the subject of housing and city planning had fascinated him. When we first met we had argued about modern architecture as much as modern literature. Roaming the streets of New York, we discovered mews and cast-iron buildings. We cared passionately about the fate of old buildings and the design of new ones. We were devoted readers of Jane Jacobs, Lewis Mumford, and Ada Louise Huxtable. Above all, housing was to us the crucial domestic problem facing America —the key to integration, to saving the cities and preserving

the countryside from suburban sprawl. Homex seemed to be
where the action was, at the front line of the housing revolution. Beyond that, it embodied the most positive goals of the
American dream—corporate profit married to a social conscience. Even I had to admit that such a company might
provide meaningful work in a way that simply making
money could not. It would merge Jerry's vocation and avoca-
tion. He could function as a lawyer, get in on the ground floor
of a new technology, and contribute to society all at once.

Jerry flew to Rochester in early November. Except for our
parents, no one else knew. It was a secret trip. I was eager
to share this horrible turn of events with friends, but Jerry
insisted it would be premature. So I kept silent, half-hoping,
like a child, that if I pretended the beast was not there, it
would go away. Perhaps Jerry would take an instant dislike
to the Stirlings. Perhaps he would be disappointed by the real
company as opposed to the paper dream. Perhaps Rochester,
as a place to live and not merely visit, would strike him as
hopelessly provincial. But none of these things happened.

Jerry was given the classic Homex tour of the assembly
line, which, we subsequently discovered, never failed to turn
skeptics into believers. Far more sophisticated men—like
HUD Secretary George Romney—became convinced they
had seen the future and it worked. Jerry's enthusiasm was
obvious. While he had reiterated to Harold Yanowitch that
only a spectacular combination of money and stock could
blast him out of the Big Apple, I knew that my husband was
a ripe fruit waiting to be plucked.

A few weeks later Yanowitch came to New York and presented Jerry with the offer. I prayed it would be too low.
Instead, it was everything Jerry had hoped for, and more.
The package included a salary of fifty thousand dollars, a
five-year employment agreement, and 12,000 options at
twelve dollars a share to be picked up over the five-year
period. Homex would pay all moving expenses and would
arrange for bank loans so that we could buy both a house and
the first of the options. Jerry was jubilant, but he dickered
about the option price, asked for a company car and 1,000

shares of the stock at the offering price when the issue became effective. By now it was obvious Wall Street was so primed for the stock that laying one's hands on a few shares would be, in the short run, like finding a satchel of money.

Yanowitch was unperturbed by the demands. He would see what he could do. He invited us to Rochester to meet the other attorneys, spend a day with a real-estate agent, and attend a dinner party at his home. The final details of the deal could be worked out at that time. Jerry agreed.

That evening I understood the nightmare was not over; it was just beginning. Barring an act of God, my husband would take the job and we would leave New York.

The choice seemed to be between seizing a great opportunity or sticking with a law practice that was, in fact, falling apart. Jerry's salary had recently been cut back. The stock market was on the verge of another major crash. The seesaw was completely tipped to one side. What did I have to counterbalance it with?

Very little. I did not have a serious career or high-paying job to call my own. I was a free-lance writer in theory only. Ten years of friendships and connections bound me to the world of book and magazine publishing, but in 1969 I was one of thousands of New York women dabbling at the edge of professionalism. Nothing concrete required my presence in New York. Only that indefinable thing called *me*—my heart, my blood, every nerve and muscle in my brain and body required New York. And that simply didn't pay the rent.

Besides, since I was ready for a new phase in my life, how could I deny a similar readiness in my husband? Jerry was thirty-five years old. He felt himself approaching that age when more options would close than open. He believed the time to make his move was now.

Intellectually I agreed that change, growth, risk, new challenges were what made life exciting. Hadn't I always reserved the greatest pity for men and women stuck in middle-aged ruts? So how could I condemn my husband to such a fate? I couldn't. Surely I was smart enough to find a part-time job in Rochester? And perhaps Jerry, relieved of the exhausting pace of New York, and the daily anxieties of a practice dependent on the vagaries of the stock market, might become a better husband and father. He assured me he would. He assured me the move would be better for all of us.

It was and is the kind of dream to which many urban, middle-class couples are susceptible. Newspapers are filled with human-interest stories of executives who flee the rat race for a life in which work and family are more in harmony. They surrender the city with all its unique pleasures, consciously opt to be out of the center of things, in return for being closer to their children and wives.

I allowed myself to fall for that dream. Partly because, with two young children, I needed a husband who had more time and emotional energy for his family, and because I had recently seen an extraordinary change in his temperament during a summer vacation away from New York.

We had rented a house on the eastern tip of Long Island. Because the new-issue market was drying up, Jerry spent three weeks with the family. Since the children had been born, we had never spent so much unbroken time together. We played tennis, barbecued, took long walks on the beach, and together observed our elder son enjoy the freedom of a front and back yard. Very ordinary moments, but never experienced by us before. The rhythm of our lives altered. Jerry was more patient with the children and more loving toward me. Connections were reestablished that we had not been aware were lost, and Jerry was more sensitive to the change than I. He talked about it a great deal. Perhaps, he wondered out loud, there was something wrong with the way we lived in New York? What was the point of long hours and a big salary if they left him emotionally drained and irritable? I had denied that New York was the villain. But now I wondered. Perhaps that happy month was a preview of things to come. Of what could be.

But it was one thing to conjure up a vision of the all-American family and quite another to contemplate a weekend in Rochester. It was the difference between imagining oneself the mother of a rosy newborn and facing the last days before childbirth. Outwardly I carried on as usual, but inwardly the dread and terror mounted until I felt almost numb.

The flight to Rochester took forty-three minutes. As long as a slow bus trip to Saks, I told myself, resisting every opportunity to look out the window. Finally, when we began our descent over Rochester, poised on the polluted banks of Lake Ontario, I peered out and had the horrifying impression the city could be seen at a glance. That, of course, is impossible. Rochester and its environs, with three quarters of a million people, is the apotheosis of suburban sprawl. It is a city of homeowners. But nothing could dissuade me from perceiving it a village the size of a Yukon trading post. As we circled for a landing, the tears began to flow, unbidden. They continued off and on for the entire weekend and vanished the moment I stepped back on the plane for New York.

Jerry was uncommonly gentle and understanding, like a father with a sick child. I stood passively as he located our bags, exchanged pleasantries with the Avis lady, and bustled about the airport. He chose a nonscenic route into town in order to show me Homex's first inner-city project. It was like taking a visitor to Manhattan via the South Bronx. The slums of Rochester, where one of the nation's first black riots had erupted, were more rural than New York's but equally depressing. Rickety frame houses stretched for miles. The Homex townhouses stood out like scrubbed faces in a crowd of miners. They were attached, two-story brick and half-timbered pseudo-Tudors. Except for a total lack of landscaping, the project might have blended into a residential section of Forest Hills. I was impressed, having envisioned God knows what kind of public-housing monstrosity. "They're really not bad," I admitted, and realized those were the first words I had uttered since we arrived.

It was a Friday night. "Downtown" Rochester was deserted. It looked like an abandoned New England mill town, the kind I had passed on my way to Cape Cod and shuddered at. Our modern box of a hotel overlooked the muddy Genesee River. Like the Seine it flowed through the center of the city, dividing East Main Street from West Main Street. On the opposite bank, a Holiday Inn was rising. Apparently, downtown Rochester was starting all over again, tearing out its decayed heart and replacing it with the usual sterile collection of government buildings and office towers. I figured any city that could boast two second-rate chain hotels as the keystone of its rebirth had to be the asshole of the world.

Saturday morning was gray and bleak. Typical Rochester weather, as I later discovered. Our real-estate agents, highly recommended by Yanowitch, turned out to be provincials of a special sort. They were an elderly Jewish couple who, I soon gathered, assumed our dreams devolved upon a split-level within walking distance of Beth El.

In fairness, I knew nothing of the rules and pitfalls of looking for a house. I knew nothing about houses. What was a center-hall colonial? Did we want a family room? What *was* a family room?

Although we tentatively voiced our preference for old houses and city living, we were led through a succession of treeless tracts. Between each stop I sobbed as unobtrusively as possible in the back seat. The only light moment came when we visited the home of a Xerox executive who was being transferred to San Francisco. (San Francisco, I thought. What bliss!) The wife looked as if she had just been stabbed in the back. Jerry and I exchanged knowing looks and laughed all the way back to the car. The joke was lost on our guides.

Late in the afternoon we cruised through a picture-book village with immaculate lawns, huge trees, and restored Federal and Greek Revival homes, and for the first time I found myself thinking that I could actually live here.

"Slow down," I shouted. "Where are we?"

"You don't want to buy a house here," our driver replied and stepped on the gas. I was too astonished to speak. Jerry looked murderous. "My wife says she likes this area," he said evenly. "Kindly pull over."

Two faces peered back at us with interest. "This is the

village of Pittsford," the husband explained.

"Too much traffic," his wife added. "Besides, mostly older people live here. Natives. . . ." There was a significant pause. "You wouldn't be *comfortable* in this atmosphere, if you know what I mean."

It had not occurred to me that restricted neighborhoods still existed. A strained silence ensued. We stated, for the record, that our neighbors' age and religious persuasion was of no interest, but it seemed hopeless and we asked to be driven back to our hotel.

I was exhausted. I wanted to sleep forever, to close my eyes and awaken in New York, in my lovely brass bed, in my snug bedroom, in my beautiful apartment which, without a breakfast nook, washer-dryer, central air conditioning, and indoor grill was my heart's desire.

"They're a cute couple," I said at last, after Jerry had stretched himself out beside me. "Makes you look forward to those sunset years."

Jerry laughed despite himself. "What I can't understand is why Harold picked them, of all people, to show us around."

"Maybe he doesn't understand you," I offered. "Or maybe it's his way of telling you he changed his mind."

"Very funny," said Jerry.

"Some joke," I replied.

It was now time to shower, change, and ready ourselves for the Yanowitch dinner. I had shopped for a week for the appropriate, conservative outfit to wear, a purple wool pantsuit and blouse. In my distressed state, I had left the blouse at home. The hell with it, I thought. Maybe they'll find me an unfit executive wife and send us packing.

We drove out East Avenue, once the city's most fashionable street and still lined with mansions of an era and scale that reminded me of Princeton's fraternity row. The Yanowitch estate fronted on East Avenue in the suburb of Pittsford, now the wealthiest and most prestigious suburb in the county. We entered a semicircular driveway through two stone pillars and pulled up before a brick residence the size of a small museum.

The Yanowitches possessed all the amenities of the super-rich: a yacht moored on Lake Seneca, horses stabled on their estate, flower and vegetable gardens, a pool, and acres of manicured lawn. Despite my New York sophistication, which occasionally exposed me to Sutton Place townhouses and Park Avenue triplexes, I was unfamiliar with this kind of semicountrified, château grandeur and prepared to dislike the formality I assumed went with it. What I found was quite unexpected. An unkempt sheepdog danced around us. Bicycles and tricycles littered our path. The front door was opened not by a maid or butler, but by a smiling, youthful figure who turned out to be our host.

It was difficult to believe Harold Yanowitch was past fifty. His skin had that ruddy glow I associated with movie stars and campaigning politicians. Small, trim, impeccably sheathed in a double-breasted Cardin suit, only his graying brown hair carefully brushed over a bald spot revealed a battle with age that had not been totally won.

Harold flashed a big, toothy smile and pumped my hand warmly.

"So, you're the evil genius," I quipped, hearing my joke turn sour in midair, but strangely pleased by my faux pas.

"Wha-a-t?" Harold was slightly hard of hearing and assumed he had misunderstood.

"I call you the evil genius," I cheerfully explained, "because you are the man who is dragging us out of New York."

"Oh yes, I see," said Harold, with a quizzical look that suggested he didn't see at all. But his wife, Joan, who joined us, understood very well. As I later discovered, she loathed Rochester, to which she had come as a young bride. Twenty years later, she was still an unregenerate New Yorker and dressed like a woman determined to dazzle. That evening she wore a pair of printed *palazzo* pajamas while the rest of us wore basic wool. Score one for Joan, I thought, chuckling at my tailored suit.

Harold and Joan were an odd pair. He was reserved, soft-spoken, and, it appeared, dispassionate, while she was a jolly whirlwind, an exuberant life force with dark, intelligent eyes and a mass of black, curly hair. Their tastes and habits were different. He rose early, watched his weight like an athlete in training, and preferred early nights. She was helpless before food, nonathletic, and moved into high gear after midnight. She invited spontaneity and frankness, and I immediately liked her for that. Joan took one look at my face, put her arm around me, and said, "Welcome to Rochester, kid." We laughed like old friends.

Their entrance hall, at the foot of a broad, circular staircase, could have comfortably fit the Mormon choir. To the right was a formal dining room, its table sparklingly set with china and crystal for dinner. Beyond us was a glassed-in summer porch and to the left, like public rooms in an old-fashioned hotel, were a series of chambers of increasing size. The last and largest was the living room where the other guests were already gathered, sipping their drinks.

The legal staff had been assembled like a well-balanced political ticket. Ultimately, it would boast two black, ex-city court judges; two Italians; two Jews; and a genuine WASP. That night the first team consisted of Thomas SantaLucia, an ex-Democratic city councilman from Buffalo, and his petite wife, Dee; Reuben Davis, the first black judge in Rochester, and his wife, Greta; Jerry, the big-city lawyer, and myself.

The central but absent figure of the evening was David Stirling. I was by now familiar with the Horatio Alger aspects of his life, how he and his brother, children of Scottish immigrants, had grown up in the slums of Toronto, how neither had finished high school, and how David had risen from apprentice to partner of a Canadian home builder before moving to the Buffalo-Rochester area where he went into business for himself. During the sixties the brothers ran a successful, conventional home-building company until, so the story went, it occurred to David to manufacture townhouses, like mobile homes, on an assembly line. He then persuaded a local group of investors, including an heir to the Western Union fortune, Harper Sibley, Jr., to finance his first modular venture, which was so successful and so artfully promoted that local bank credit was extended to the infant

company, an assembly line built, and more ambitious operations launched. Since 1968 Homex had manufactured 773
modular dwelling units and had attracted the attention of
HUD and various housing authorities, notably one in Akron,
whose federally financed mission was to provide low-cost
housing for the poor and elderly. Now Homex was in the
midst of another plant expansion and eying national markets
and methods of distribution. The public offering would
finance its leap into the major leagues.

David Stirling was thirty-six; his brother a mere thirty-one.
Their meteoric success was the stuff of which fables are
made. From the very beginning, Yanowitch impressed upon
his recruits that Homex was not just a new company, but a
magic circle. At the heart of this kingdom lay the young
David—a great man, a humble man, a self-made man, a
genius.

I had hoped to meet David Stirling at the Yanowitch home,
to independently assess his intelligence and charm. Instead
I made do, like a lady-in-waiting, with snippets of information about the royal family. I was intrigued to hear, for example, that the two brothers had gone to Scotland to find brides
and that the entire Stirling clan now lived next door to one
another in a compound outside of Avon, New York, called
Hickory Hill.

"You mean like the Kennedys' 'Hickory Hill'?" I inquired.

"Yes," replied Harold. "I guess so." The coincidence had
never occurred to him.

Inevitably, and largely for my benefit, since my reluctance
to move to Rochester was an open secret, the conversation
turned to what life in Rochester was really like. My first
question was about the weather. I hated the cold almost as
much as I hated flying, and I inquired whether it was true
that Rochester, like Syracuse, was in the middle of the snow-
belt.

"Not at all," said Harold, echoing what I have come to
regard as the standard Chamber-of-Commerce line. "Buffalo
and Syracuse have far worse weather."

Dee SantaLucia, a lifelong resident of Buffalo, agreed that

nothing could be worse than Buffalo's weather.

"You know, Harold," Reuben purred, as though on cue, "I can't remember the last time I had to plough my driveway." Harold seconded the thought. "I can even recall golfing in January."

I was touchingly innocent. Golfing in January sounded swell.

Dinner was served by women in gray uniforms, white aprons, and caps. I was seated to the right of Harold, or "H" as his wife called him, and to the left of Tommy SantaLucia, who had already begun his year-long commute between Buffalo and Rochester. He too was a city boy, and it was apparent that even a Buffalonian found downtown Rochester a joke. We got along famously.

Harold was more difficult to draw out. For him it was a working night. His job was to appear friendly, to present Rochester, Homex, and the Stirlings in their most favorable light, and to convey the impression that our husbands were about to assume positions of extreme power and authority, while we, as their wives, would enter society at a level reflecting their prestige.

Perhaps because Harold had always operated in a small community where a handful of businessmen did, in fact, run the town, he believed, as no New Yorker can, that the way he conducted his life was highly visible, that his private and public activities were inextricably bound. Harold was a native Rochesterian in a town teeming with executive transients. He extolled the city's parks, the beauty of the Finger Lakes and urged me, when I moved up, to "take advantage of the great outdoors." He himself was a physical fitness nut. He often rode his horses or biked before breakfast and had recently taken up skiing. "Your kids will love the life," he assured me.

There were moments during the evening when I had to remind myself where I was and what I was doing there. Although I asked questions, observed the men, strained for every nuance, glance, and shift of tone that might reveal who these strangers were, part of me felt anesthetized. And while this ritual of being the recruited executive's wife was unique to my experience, something about the occasion was naggingly familiar. It was only when we were putting on our coats that my double vision snapped into focus.

The SantaLucias were returning to Buffalo and we to New York the next day. Harold seemed determined to end the night on an up-beat note. "None of you will have any regrets," he murmured. "Believe me, this is a great moment, a great opportunity." Speaking directly to Mrs. SantaLucia, he added, "You mark my words, Dee. Your husband will be a millionaire someday."

Dee shrieked with laughter and shook her head with disbelief. Then I heard the lines that had been reverberating in my brain all night. They had haunted Willy Loman in *Death of a Salesman*, and now the eerie refrain of Willy's brother Ben, haunted me.

> William, when I walked into the jungle, I was seventeen. When I walked out I was twenty-one. And by God I was rich.

Harold was our Ben. He was the figure of our collective fantasies, urging us away from home, onto a new continent, whispering in our ears, "You could walk out rich. Rich!"

Winter–Spring 1969–1970

CHAPTER III

Although in my own mind it was merely a formality, Jerry accepted the offer the first week of December. It had been sweetened with the opportunity to purchase an additional 525 shares of stock at the opening price whenever Homex went public. He was to begin work in Avon—a small town twenty miles south of Rochester where the factory and executive offices were located—a month later.

I gave way to the flow of events as though they were a natural force over which I had no control. I accepted them as I would have a tornado, bitterly, uncomprehendingly, but resigned to a fate that had passed out of my hands. There was no confrontation between me and Jerry. It was understood I did not want to move but would never say no. It was understood that despite my feminist dreams of an egalitarian marriage, I was still a conventional wife unprepared to explore the radical alternatives to the problem of job mobility. Whither thou goest. For better or for worse. Through thick and thin.

When Jerry announced our impending move to Joshua, I was in the next room weeping, just like that woman in the Homerica moving company ad, the one with the wife sprawled across the bed, misery furrowing her brow. For years I had noticed that ad with uneasiness. There was something distasteful about the picture and headline beneath it:

A BIG PROMOTION, $4,000 MORE IN SALARY, AND HIS
WIFE IS IN TEARS. It suggested there was something wrong
with this woman because she didn't share her husband's tri-
umphant promotion. It implied a certain female irrationality.
The ad was humiliating not simply because it reduced
women to the level of a cliché, but because it offered a con-
sumer-solution to a complicated emotional crisis. "Give the
lady a nice house, and she'll be shipshape in no time." That
was the abhorrent message, and I resented it.

But in fact, once the big decision had been taken, it became my responsibility to grapple with all the secondary
decisions that inevitably followed. That was my realm—the
kingdom of practical details—and for a while it gave me the
illusion that I was again in command of my life.

The first issue was, indeed, a house. Here I put my foot
down. I would not move to temporary quarters in a strange
town with no friends in the middle of winter. Let Jerry commute to Avon and continue to house hunt. At best, we would
arrive with the spring thaw.

Even Joshua revealed an anxiety about where we would
live. Incapable of understanding what the word *move* implied, he only wanted to know if it would be like going to a
new apartment. No, Jerry replied. It would probably be a
house. Would we all be together? Joshua asked. Beyond that,
it seemed, nothing mattered.

But I knew what a profound wrench it would be, suddenly
remembering the unhappy years that followed my move
from Washington, D.C. to New York at the age of eight. It
was a period in my life I had tried very hard to forget.

As an adult I now recognized that my bewilderment and
despair reflected my mother's unhappiness as much as my
own. In Washington, she had been one of a small circle of
Italian refugees, all struggling to adjust to a new language,
culture, and a life of modest means. They had been relatively
prosperous in Italy, with maids, nurses for the children, surrounded by family, but Americans regarded them as lower-
middle-class refugees with heavy accents. At least in Washington they had had each other. But in New York my mother,

without friends, was catapulted into a world of wealth and social pretensions. My father was constantly traveling. His salary did not stretch as far as it had in Washington, so my mother was stuck in an apartment with two daughters, one eight, the other six months. Recently she had admitted to me what a nightmare those first New York years were, but we never discussed what was equally obvious, its effect on her children and marriage. Resentments were formed that took twenty years to surface.

My first concern, then, was not to let the move disrupt my son's life as it had disrupted mine. Joshua would experience a sense of loss, and it was up to me to prepare him for the good and the bad. I had to be positive—if not gay, then at least calm and unruffled whenever the subject came up. Which was why I had bowed out of the initial disclosure. But a few days later I rushed into the apartment with a load of library books, about the city mouse and the country mouse, about Johnny who missed his friends but soon made new ones. I bought various maps of the United States, spread them out on the living room floor, and made a game of finding the black dot that represented our future home.

But in private my fantasies revolved around composing a generational novel entitled "Leaving Home." The same pattern of reluctant departure had hounded all of us—my mother fleeing Nazi Germany; my father fleeing fascist Italy; all of us declared enemy aliens in England and forced to find a new home. My uprooting began when I was eight months old, an infant in my grandmother's arms. I remembered nothing of those early pilgrimages, though they were told and retold a thousand times. But perhaps a Freudian would say they explained my present horror of change, that my love of New York, which I always believed a sign of great strength, was an irrational emotion common to adults without secure roots.

Thinking about the novel gave me the intellectual perspective I needed to deal with what was happening to me. How could I compare my measly 350-mile displacement to the Jewish Diaspora? It was an old trick of mine, theorizing about a character's dilemmas, detaching myself from myself instead of giving into feelings that might break me open. Perhaps if I had ranted and raved, if I had given into my emotions, we would not have moved. But that involved violating an image of myself as "mature," "controlled" and, yes, "superior." I was no run-of-the-mill female hysteric. I was fighting the old notion that women are *emotional*, which was accepted as a sign of their inferiority. Well, this chick was going to prove otherwise. She was going to be tough.

Our friends reacted to the news as though we had betrayed New York. My feelings exactly. "You, of all couples," they murmured. But once over the shock, an unforeseen polarity of attitude emerged. The men were excited for Jerry. Enormously impressed. Convinced the decision was right. The kids would be better off. New York was falling apart. Eleanor would adjust. It was the opportunity of a lifetime. And so on.

The women were less sanguine. What are you going to *do* up there? Find a part-time job, I guess. But at what? Silence. I wonder what *I* would do in your situation? Silence. Of course it's a great job for Jerry . . . and the conversation would trail off.

All of my friends were vocal advocates of the women's movement. Many had married late, and most had waited until their late twenties or early thirties before having children. None of us thought of ourselves as ordinary housewives. We all believed it was important to spend time with our children during their earliest years, but once they were in school, we could and should resume our careers. There was a great deal of talk about the propitious moment to abandon the playground scene, about au-pair girls, and housekeepers, and how it was working out for Jane's children when *she* went back to work. None of us was content to join the League of Women Voters and stay home.

And yet, aside from constantly discussing feminist issues, we were not activists. We were women who had known the score long before the movement became official. We had never bought the feminine mystique, so we thought, and in the way of old revolutionaries, smiled benignly but passively at the contemporary scene.

Like all nonradicals, we accommodated the movement to our lives, instead of the other way around. We had no need to rock the boat. We had married enlightened men. They might not share the domestic chores as much as we wished, but intellectually they were on our side. That's what counted. So no one suggested I refuse to move. Not only was it unthinkable, but also in a social circle peculiarly free of executive transients no one felt personally threatened by my misfortune. Like cancer, it would never happen to them.

Unexpectedly a near-stranger gave me my first insight into the real problems lurking ahead. She was a lay psychologist leading a discussion group of Montessori parents on problems of child rearing. I had joined in the spirit of one who believes in preventive health care. But one evening, thinking here was a chance to get expert advice on easing the change for Joshua, I brought up the subject of our move. Halfway through my opening sentence, I burst into tears. I was mortified. The other adults were embarrassed. A long silence ensued until the psychologist, in a rush of feeling, poured out her story. A few years before, her husband, a college teacher, had moved her and the family from New York to a small town in Pennsylvania. It was in coal country. Ugly. Cold. Isolated. Nowheresville. For two years she had struggled to adjust, but it was hopeless. This past fall she had moved back, by herself, to a one-room apartment in Greenwich Village. She pursued her profession during the week and commuted back to Pennsylvania by bus on weekends. A housekeeper looked after her teen-age children. Sometimes they visited her in New York.

Everyone was astonished, but for me the revelation was like a slow immersion in ice water. Here was this conventional-looking, middle-aged woman who had said, "The hell with the rules," and left. She was neither a radical feminist nor one of the beautiful people, like Mary Wells, who jetted between New York and Dallas. She was an ordinary person who confirmed both my worst fears of what it could be like out there and my suspicion that the private hell of such women was one of the best-kept secrets of our age. It was the first in a long line of harrowing stories I was to hear, but I was particularly fascinated by this woman's solution to her problem. It was a possibility I had never considered.

My parents and Jerry's parents had not a moment's doubt about the opportunity. Like all immigrants they believed—were themselves living proof—that in America a hard-working, talented man could rise. Now it was Jerry's turn to seize the day. They were dazzled by his salary, but even more by the public verification of success it bestowed. My father-in-law had sometimes expressed doubts about his second son. He wasn't aggressive enough. He was too honest. He didn't plan for the future or put aside money. My father, once the youngest professor of economics in Italy, had not seen a Supreme Court appointment in Jerry's future. But now they could say, Jerome Dienstag, the corporate lawyer. In their eyes this 170-pound weakling had finally become a man.

My mother and mother-in-law were uneasy with my tears. Since they had both been wrenched from their families, they understood my sorrow, but for them the circumstances had been the threat of poverty and war. By comparison, my uprooting would be as free of stress as theirs had been traumatic. What did I have to complain about? Wasn't a wife's duty beside her husband? Wasn't I proud of Jerry? Didn't I realize how lucky I was to be married to a man who would be making fifty thousand dollars a year? The gap between us as women was unbridgeable.

For Jerry it was a joyful December. He had the pleasure of being the first to abandon a sinking law firm. He met old friends for leisurely lunches, to say good-bye and preen a bit. He strolled the preholiday streets of New York feeling, for once, that security and inner calm that comes with success. The approach of a new year had often sunk him into a where-am-I-going gloom. How glorious to be free of all that.

Everyone toasted Jerry on New Year's Eve. And then, without our having given it much thought, he packed a few bags and was off to begin his new life.

In January of 1970 Stirling Homex was in the midst of a frenzied recruitment drive. Newly hired engineers, salesmen, and systems experts poured into Avon from all over the country, leaving wives to sell houses and children to finish school years. Like Jerry, they commuted home on the weekends and lived, during the week, in a modular townhouse development built and owned by the Stirlings and located a few miles from the plant.

Jerry's first month on the job was relatively eventless. He was learning about the business, reading files, familiarizing himself with projects, and meeting other executives in the organization. Basically, he was readying himself for the SEC's Letter of Comments on the preliminary prospectus. It was like waiting for D day. The growth of the company depended on a successful stock offering. Nothing was more important to the Stirlings and Yanowitch than the fate of the prospectus.

When the Letter of Comments arrived on February 5 it was, in Jerry's words, "an eleven-page nightmare." The SEC raised many substantive objections to the company's accounting practices that prompted rounds of meetings between Homex's inside legal and financial staff, its New York counsel (Shea, Gallop, Climenko & Gould), the attorneys for the underwriter (Simpson, Thatcher & Bartlett), and the underwriters themselves. Jerry shuttled back and forth between Rochester and New York, then flew to Washington for a crucial face-to-face conference between the SEC staff and Homex's phalanx of lawyers.

The purpose of the meeting was to convince the SEC of Homex's legitimacy and special problems as a new business. No one, it turned out, was better suited to this task than Harold Yanowitch. Jerry later confided to me that, despite the presence of abler legal minds, it was Harold's missionary-like belief in Homex that moved the SEC to waive a number of its key objections to the prospectus. Now the race was on to rewrite and go effective, hopefully within the week.

It was like old times. Jerry was back in New York, working around the clock, and virtually living at the printers. Financial printers are masters of seduction. In a fiercely competitive, highly lucrative business, they not only offer quick, effi-

cient service but also a setting that makes the ordinary lawyer feel like a God. For a few days they fulfill the male dream
of power and wealth by providing chauffeur-driven limou-
sines, free drinks, night-and-day flunkies, and exquisite food
in restaurants where the owner falls all over himself to be
helpful. Every lawyer who has ever been through the routine
remembers it for a lifetime: the restaurant table with a
phone; a Cadillac or Lincoln waiting at the curb; being
whisked through the city at dawn.

I knew the scene and was prepared for that moment when
Jerry, giddy from sleeplessness, returned home like a warrior
from battle. But this time he had reason to believe himself
a hero. An unexpected drama had taken place.

At two in the morning, hours before the prospectus was to
be flown to Washington, a young man representing the underwriters, with whom Jerry had been hammering out the
final draft, suddenly began asking a lot of fundamental questions about the company. Why were there so many uninstalled modules sitting outside the plant? What about this
footnote? Was it accurate? And so on. Jerry became alarmed
and furious. Was this kid trying to torpedo the deal? Jerry
blew up. He accused the young man of not having done his
homework, of lacking faith, of pettiness, of bad judgment, of
everything he could think of. It was an Academy Award
performance. The startled creature backed down. The prospectus went through, but Jerry felt uneasy. Perhaps he had
permanently alienated the underwriters and acted unjudi-
ciously. He phoned Yanowitch, who was staying at the Plaza
with the Stirlings, to tell him what happened. Ten minutes
later David Stirling was on the phone. He couldn't have been
more reassuring. Jerry felt euphoric. He woke me up to re-
late the entire tale.

"And do you know what David's final words to me were?"

"No, what?" I mumbled.

"He said, 'You did absolutely the right thing. If I had been
there, I would have punched the guy in the fucking mouth.' "

The next day a private jet whisked the Stirlings, Yanowitch, the president of R. W. Pressprich, and my husband

back to Rochester. The plane's pilot was ex-astronaut Frank Borman. He had been touted onto Homex as an investment by his good friend Ross Perot, the Texas millionaire whose Electronic Data Systems had also gone public through Pressprich.

The prospectus was processed with lightning speed. Within forty-eight hours of its delivery to Washington, the stock was declared effective. Offered at $16.50 a share, its first trade was at $33. Within two weeks, the stock had flown to $50. By March 1970, a month after its debut, it had risen to $51.75 per share, or 250 times earnings, and this in a generally bear market.

According to Jerry, Homex executives were so riveted by news of the stock that no one could concentrate on daily office work. In New York I was besieged by congratulatory calls. And by the way, did Jerry know where one could get a hold of a few shares?

Seven days later, David and Bill Stirling, proudly escorted by their father, returned to New York to receive a check for $6.5 million. Jerry prepared the closing papers and witnessed their alchemization into cash. The moment was immortalized by *Forbes* magazine. The May 1 issue ran a photograph of the two seated brothers with "million-dollar smiles." Standing between them was an unidentified stranger, my husband, his lips struggling to surpress an undignified grin. The story next to the picture was headlined, "There's Nothing Like a Dream."

Forbes called David Stirling "the Henry Ford of the housing industry," and Homex "the salvation of the housing crisis." Jerry's lawyerlike reservations about the future were swept away by the continuing waves of good news, which included Homex's recent selection by HUD as an "Operation Breakthrough" winner. The company had signed a $3.6 million contract to manufacture and install a thirteen-story steel-and-concrete high rise in Memphis, Tennessee. The two hundred-unit building was to be erected by a revolutionary method, hydraulic jacks, which had been developed by Homex engineers.

I pretended to share Jerry's enthusiasm but was privately

unmoved by the glamour-atmosphere surrounding the stock, and what I could not help feeling were manic predictions about its future. So Frank Borman piloted a jet for the Stirlings. Big deal. The plane ride sounded like a junket for grown-up groupies. Besides, as anyone knew who had lived through the roller coaster of the sixties, high-fliers had a way of coming down faster than they went up. I would have preferred words of cautious optimism.

Of course my reservations were partly due to an irrational hostility toward this company that was ruining my life. But I had also come to believe in the fundamental irrationality of the stock market. It did not rise and fall according to the real merits of a business. It functioned on rumor and whim. For us, Homex was a long-term investment. We could not make a killing and run. The first of Jerry's options could not be purchased for a year, and who knew where the stock would be then? The dangers were many: that the mysterious love affair between Wall Street and Homex would end; that the bear market of 1970 would ultimately discourage all speculative investments; and that Homex would become so obsessed with its paper value, would devote so much time to its public relations that it would fail to pursue its real mission in life, which was to sell houses.

Jerry had little to say about Avon and Rochester, except that he had never seen so much snow in his life. Even for natives, that winter's 150.4 inches was a near record, but for a man with few friends, living in a sparsely furnished apartment in a village so backward its only movie house stopped the show to change reels, it was exceptionally depressing. Mostly, Jerry watched TV and subsisted on a bachelor diet of peanuts, martinis, TV dinners, and candy. By March he had put on fifteen pounds and couldn't wait until we moved up.

In late February I made another two-day trip to Rochester. This time, guided by an energetic, new broker, I remained reasonably dry-eyed and found our home. It was a formal, three-story brick dwelling, in the heart of the city, off East Avenue, and two doors away from a landmark Frank Lloyd

Wright "prairie" house. Built around 1910, its interior bore an uncanny resemblance to our New York apartment, with high ceilings, dentellated moldings, inlaid floors, and enough space to accommodate our massive furniture. The living and dining rooms were of equal size, each with a bay window. In addition to a large kitchen, there was a generous pantry, small playroom, and den. A magnificent staircase spiraled up to four bedrooms, and a back staircase led to the third floor, where three additional rooms had once housed servants. It was set on a corner plot with an enormous sweep of lawn and, in the rear, a hedged-in play area, already furnished with a swing and slide set.

Far grander than anything I had envisaged and comparatively cheap, I asked the broker why, fearing some major plumbing flaw. The explanation had less to do with the house than the flight to the suburbs. People were afraid to live in town, especially since the mid-sixties riots. On top of that, mortgage money was tight, and Xerox had recently transferred two hundred top executives to Stamford, creating a glut on the market. The house, originally listed at about seventy thousand dollars, had remained unsold and empty for a year. It was a genuine buy. We made an offer of forty-five thousand dollars, and a few days later it was ours.

I was surprised by my lack of feeling for the place. Objectively, it was nothing short of grand. In New York it would have been considered a palace. If it had occupied a choice lot on West Seventy-ninth Street, I would have spent the next ten years of my life turning it into a showcase. But as a psychiatrist once observed, "Moving is a severe trauma, probably as great as divorce." If you have invested the deepest emotions in one home and experienced its loss, you are incapable of repeating that emotional commitment. Certainly not right away. The last thing I wanted was to become *attached.* I also recognized that furnishing one's nest is for many women a pseudo-career, one of the many traps society sets for intelligent females who would be better advised to prepare for that moment when the nest is empty. I had already spent too many hours of my life trudging through fabric showrooms, eschewing professional help because I believed it important my home reflect *me*, down to the last knob on the kitchen cabinets. That phase was over. I would make the house livable and forget about it. So I called up a part-time decorator friend, flew her up to Rochester for a day, and by the end of the week decided everything from room colors to kitchen renovations. We hired a contractor and insisted the work be completed within the month. Despite dozens of crises, our schedule was met.

On April 20, a day before my husband's thirty-fifth birthday, the moving van settled in front of our apartment building. We were about to become a statistic, four more among the estimated 40 million Americans who change residences every year and whose migration, lacking frontiers, is one of the least-understood social phenomenons of our times.

Our departure was marked by a final bit of New York drama. In the middle of the afternoon a flying squad of policemen rushed the building in pursuit of an armed burglar who had been spotted on the roof. I was on the sidewalk supervising the movers; Jerry and the children were inside the apartment. There was the distinct possibility that the trapped man might seize a hostage. Since the door to our apartment had been open all day, there was the equally distinct possibility that the fugitive, rushing down the stairs, might fling himself into it. I waited, wondering if it was possible that during the last hour of our last day in New York, one of those random acts of violence would, at last, strike home.

The police had ordered me into the van. I stood at the top of the ramp next to one of the moving men.

"You're lucky to be getting out of this jungle," he said.

"I guess so," I replied, choking back tears whose meaning I no longer understood.

Within a half-hour it was all over. A young man in handcuffs was hustled into a police car.

"*I'd* be afraid to live in this neighborhood," the barrel-chested mover confessed, as we rode back to the eighth floor.

"I know how you feel," I admitted. "But you see, the crazy thing is, I'm afraid *not* to."

CHAPTER IV

Dismantling, compressing, and transporting one's household, whether across the street or hundreds of miles away, is a profoundly unnerving moment—a breath between past and future, a step into the void where old routines are shattered and new ones barely perceived. It is a time when even people not given to backward glances understand an era in their life is over, its pleasures and pains forever identified with the rooms in which they took place. As I walked the apartment for the last time, I remembered the morning I had brought my first son into it. I remembered a Fourth of July party we had given because of the view from our windows of the Hudson River fireworks. I remembered the hundreds of nights I had sat in the living room watching the sunsets, the changing patterns of light and cloud, and the evening the lights went out in Manhattan when I had diapered the baby on a radiator cover by candlelight. I was too choked with memories to speak. Only when we were in the back of a cab, taking that familiar, short ride to my parents' apartment did I finally give into the tears that had been threatening all day. Afterward I felt better, almost cleansed. I was ready, I thought, to start all over again.

Traditionally, it has been the job of "the little woman" to render order out of chaos, to banish anxieties by recreating, as quickly as possible, the familiar furniture and rituals of home. Like so many women I accepted that role and prided myself on being a superb organizer. As a child I had shown no talent in that direction. I was a teen-age slob, forgetful, distracted, and thoroughly indifferent to domestic chores. My mother demanded very little of me and I gave even less. But gradually, and no doubt partially because I had married a man who flinched at the sight of an unmade bed and equated an unpressed dress with moral degeneracy, I had changed. By the time of our move, I shared my husband's compulsions about neatness, cleanliness, and punctuality. I couldn't relax if the apartment was a mess; couldn't go to bed

if the kitchen contained an unwashed dish, was forever reor-
ganizing closets, picking up toys, straightening up—a monument to efficiency. Before moving, I read all the books on
How to Do It Right. I labeled cartons, remembered to pack
a set of sheets, pillowcases, and towels last, set aside toys for
the children to play with, arranged for our old phone to be
disconnected and our new one to be installed, for meters to
be read and our diaper service stopped. But by the end of our
first week in Rochester, my illusion of control was shattered.
Nothing went as planned.

To begin with, the truck broke down on the Thruway. We
spent the first night in a hotel. When the van finally lum-
bered up to our front door, in the midst of an incredible heat
wave, I discovered not a window in the house opened. The
washing machine received our sweaty traveling clothes with
a groan, then gave out. The dishwasher stood mute. The
shower turned icy when a toilet was flushed. It began to
dawn on me that we had been had, but good.

In New York the moving man eagerly bidding for the job
had assured me his workers would unload, unpack, and put
away our fragile belongings, so that damages could be
claimed on the spot. I had been misinformed. They would
unwrap. Period. The house began to look like bargain day at
Macy's.

Jerry took one day off from work after our arrival and,
attaché case in hand, fled back out to Avon with undisguised
relief. It was then I discovered the true meaning of that
innocuous phrase, "setting up a home." My husband had
simply switched commuter routes; traded one air-condi-
tioned office for another. Everything else was left to me. I
was the one who figured out where things went and put them
there. Jerry was too tired at night to do much more than
arrange his socks and assemble the crib. I was the one who
found new schools, doctors, baby-sitters, shopping centers,
parks, plumbers, electricians, carpenters, and that endless
parade of repairmen without whom the resumption of a normal life would have been impossible. Between Jerry and me
we could just about change a light bulb. Hanging pictures

brought us close to blows. Except for the Yellow Pages and Joan Yanowitch, who called me daily to feed me lists of information, I was totally isolated and more afraid of my car than my isolation.

Everyone has a knack for something. Mine is for being slightly out of step. When my peers were wearing saddle shoes and white socks, I preferred black tights and Capezios. When my college dorm echoed with the sounds of Mantovani, I played Monteverdi. When it was considered almost un-American not to own or drive a car, I crusaded for mass transportation. And just when my ecology-minded friends were trading in their Chevies for ten-speed collapsible Moultons, we became a two-car family.

Technically I possessed a driver's license, but my first solo in the backwoods of Long Island had ended with a head-on crash into a tree, and I had never quite recovered my confidence. In New York it hadn't mattered. There would never be a car pool in my future. But in Rochester it was my life line to the outside world.

We had been told a family *needed* a station wagon, a bit of advice I now rate on a par with joining the PTA to meet people in a new town. So one spring evening, several weeks after our move, Jerry turned up with a secondhand, maroon 1967 Dodge station wagon that looked like an amphibious assault ship. Backing it out of our narrow garage provoked recurring nightmares. Driving it was worse. Oncoming cars seemed to have the word *death* scrawled across their front bumpers. Visions of mutilated bodies—mostly mine—kept me hugging the edge of the road at 25 mph. Later on, like the poorest country boy, I would understand why freedom begins with four wheels. I would come to enjoy cruising the highways and careening down country lanes to the bouncy strains of "American Pie." But then I was both afraid and terribly ashamed that a five-minute drive to the supermarket left me shaky at the knees.

Not that I had anyone to see. While Jerry plunged into a structured life, where secretaries, lunch companions, and a company-leased car complete with drones who "took care of it" effortlessly fell his way, I was living in almost total isolation, experiencing what has come to be known as culture shock. I had an acute case.

At first I didn't notice. I was too busy ushering repairmen in and out of the house, nursing both children back to health (despite the last-minute checkups they both had in New York), lining shelves, and unpacking thousands of books. But gradually these chores diminished, and I began to realize Joshua had no playmates (the nearest playground was bafflingly empty), I had no friends, and the only human being to ring my doorbell was the Fuller Brush man. Although we lived in the city, there was no observable street life. Instead of people and shops and other women out strolling with their children, I was surrounded by grass and silence from nine to five.

What had I imagined? At the very least, friendly neighbors and curious children knocking on the front door. Where were all those women with cups of sugar who sweetened small-town living? As far as I could tell they had emigrated to New York, where strangers on buses displayed more warmth toward a mother with two children than anyone on my block.

I had, of course, read about women in my position, isolated in their fancy homes, newly arrived in a community and without a clue as to how to make connections. I thought I had empathized with their situation, when actually I scorned their lack of resources and imagination. Now, as I stared out the window at the empty sidewalk, the only sound that of a lawnmower blocks away, I understood the paralysis of will, the dribbling away of good intentions, the lack of confidence and the depression that could transform a capable woman into a passive female. Even the simplest tasks seemed overwhelming. Wandering through vast, wide-aisled supermarkets, I felt disoriented, almost drugged. It took me hours to choose groceries that in New York I had snapped up in minutes. The days unwound like a slow-motion dream.

At night I would wait for Jerry to come home like an invalid for the doctor's visit. What did you do today? Who did you see? What did you have for lunch? What did you talk about at lunch? If he worked late, I flew into a rage.

Sometimes, after dinner, before it got dark, Jerry and I would walk around the yard, surveying our property. We didn't know what else to do with it. We had no lawn furniture, no garden tools, no croquet set.

"Well, it's all ours," Jerry would say, proud but disbelieving.

"Yes, so it is," I would say, hating it. The bushes, the grass, the weeds intimidated me. Everything I had learned, all my savvy urban skills were useless here. I bought a bunch of house plants, hung them around the living room window just as I had in New York, and tried to ignore the garden.

The children also ignored the garden. Joshua, who had reveled in running around the playgrounds of New York, was not enticed by the swing set, the truck tire roped to our maple tree or the brand-new two-wheeler we had bought for his birthday in May. He clung to his old Montessori workbooks and "Curious George" records the way I clung to my *New Yorker, New York Times, New York Review of Books,* and *New York* subscriptions. Finally I enrolled him in a day camp, which left me, during the afternoons when Jesse napped, lonelier than ever.

It was during one of those eternal afternoons of early summer, after a tomblike silence descended upon the house, that I said to myself, okay, enough, you've got to pull yourself together, get aggressive, call strangers, do something. I took that first, excruciatingly difficult step toward others which, even thinking about it now, makes my palms sweaty. I marched into the kitchen and picked up the phone. Hi! You may not remember me, but Joan Yanowitch introduced us the other day. . . . To my amazement, it worked. What I had failed to understand was that in a small town a new face is like a breath of fresh air. People are so sick of the same crowd that, given a chance, they will sweep you into their lives with relief.

I invited women with children the same age as Jesse to the house. I gave a dinner party for the three couples I knew. I waylaid a neighbor in her backyard. Gradually, and with Joan Yanowitch as my main connection, a thin circle of acquaintances developed.

I also found a soul mate in the wife of another Homex executive whose uprooting had been more traumatic than mine. Not only had she been wrenched from New York, but also from an ideal part-time job it had taken her years of juggling baby-sitters and going back to graduate school to land. She had arrived in Rochester the previous fall, friendless, with three children under six, and a husband who traveled more than he stayed home. She had barely made it through the winter. Like characters out of *Three Sisters* we spent long afternoons reminiscing about New York, dreaming of that moment when we would return. She was convinced our exile was temporary. In the meantime she commiserated with familiar symptoms of distress, not the least of which was constant illness. Colds lingered, allergies reappeared, and I coughed and wheezed like someone with an advanced case of emphysema. Absolutely normal for Rochester, my friend observed. Her own home resembled an outpatient clinic. I was not convinced. What's wrong with me, I demanded of my doctor, hoping for some specific villain like Genesee ragweed. He prescribed tranquilizers. I was insulted, protested, but took my first Valium and floated home.

By midsummer our application to a tennis club was accepted. I loved tennis but had mixed feelings about joining a "club," which had always represented a way of life and exclusivity I disapproved of. Venturing into that sea of tanned bodies and ruffled whites intensified my sense of being an outsider—the city girl surrounded by suburban matrons. My instinctive reaction was to recoil as if from the enemy. But despite my snobberies, it was an alternative to empty days. Whenever I could find a partner and baby-sitter, I played.

Occasionally a new friend would invite me to her house and pool. There would be other women. We would loll about, talking, watching the children, munching on cheese and crackers. I was grateful for the company, pleased to be sharing this privileged existence, but inwardly terrified it would be the shape of my new life. Would I gradually sink into the indolence of the rich in a world devoid of black faces, old faces, poor people, and even working people? Would I divide my time between housekeeping, volunteer work, shopping, and a game of tennis? None of the women I met worked. They were intelligent, well-educated, constant travelers, but curiously untouched by politics, by Kent State or the antiwar movement, which was obsessing my friends in New York. They knew almost nothing about women's lib. Tell us about it, they would say. But how could I? It was like the joke about the black man who, having heard there was a nigger on the commuter train, looked around him anxiously and said, "Where? Where? Where?"

When New York friends called and asked, "What's it like?" I would reply, "Like being on vacation." Not unpleasant, but unreal and impermanent, a pause from the business of life. Sometimes I would wonder why there wasn't sand in the kitchen, as there had been in all my other summer houses. And when were the winter people coming back?

I made a few desultory attempts to find a job. Perhaps local TV stations would be interested in adding a book or movie critic to their news shows? They were. I was interviewed, but nothing came of it. Rona Barrett was more what they had in mind. So I drifted along until a day in late August when Jerry was in New York on business and my mother in town for a visit. Since we had already covered the normal "sights"—the art museum, planetarium, university, and what I dryly referred to as "boutique row," we drove out to the tennis club. I was unaware that a fashion show was taking place around the pool, but as we walked through the parking lot toward the courts, I heard a female voice over a loudspeaker. "Now here's a lovely dress for patio and beach wear," the voice crooned. As a murmur of approval went up from the unseen crowd, something inside me snapped. I began to shake and sweat like someone without food who suddenly realizes she is on the verge of starving to death. My God, I thought, that could be me in there. That could be me forever. I had to get out. I rushed back home, dashed upstairs to the bedroom phone, and closed the door on my bewildered mother saying I had an important business call to make. I dialed the number of a chain of suburban newspapers. It was my last hope and I had been putting off the call for weeks. The publisher was out, would I care to make an appointment? I would. Within a few weeks I had the job of part-time cultural reporter. Desperation had driven me back to where I belonged.

Fall 1970

CHAPTER V

By fall I seemed to be thriving. I even had myself convinced.

Joshua was ensconced in a full-day, open-classroom primary, of the sort I had read about in *The New Republic,* but never hoped to find in Rochester, New York. A two-day-a-week baby-sitter had been found and quickly engaged through a want ad in the Sunday paper; I was ready to reenter the world of paid work.

When I first called Andrew Wolfe, editor-publisher of the Genesee Valley Newspapers, I offered my services as a book reviewer. In retrospect it was an absurd proposition, like inquiring of a family on food stamps whether they'd like to hire a French tutor. But I was totally naïve about the economics of the newspaper business and believed any self-respecting journal required a book critic. As a casual reader of one of Wolfe's five suburban weeklies, *The Brighton-Pittsford Post,* I thought I detected a cultural patina totally absent from the colorless, conservative Gannett press. It featured a gourmet-food page, antiques column, and even reprinted Feiffer's weekly cartoon. Wolfe's papers looked classier than either of the city dailies. They were better laid out, beautifully printed and overflowing with quality advertising. So I assumed the enterprise was a kind of patrician, provincial *Village Voice.*

My instinct was half correct. Wolfe had a soft spot for the

arts. His eminent position in the community was not only due to his publishing power, but also to his role in preserving "historic" Pittsford and his activities on behalf of both a local arts council and the New York State Council on the Arts, to which he had been appointed by Governor Rockefeller. As it turned out, he had been searching for a reporter to cover the cultural scene. It was a field I knew precious little about, but during my first interview I assured Wolfe that as an ex-New Yorker I was probably better equipped to judge professionalism in the arts than any mere native. Oddly enough, instead of taking offense, he agreed. He liked the idea of an outsider surveying the turf. Most Rochesterians did. It seemed my knee-jerk snobbery toward the provinces was only matched by a local inferiority complex as wide and deep as the Erie Canal.

I have always done well at job interviews. It's an art like any other. But inevitably, after the bull-shit session is over and the prize mine, I am overwhelmed with the certainty that I will fail. It was one thing to *say* I could review dance, theater, music, art, books, and movies and quite another to actually do it. But the real question was, could I still write, and with a weekly deadline? I hadn't touched a typewriter in two years. And I had always been a painfully slow writer. But surprisingly, my first story on an international film festival to be held in Rochester that fall practically wrote itself. Gone was the fear. Gone were the old self-doubts. Gone was the knowledge that if I turned an awkward or banal phrase, every writer and editor in New York would forever rank me a mediocre hack. Nothing hung in the balance, I told myself, except a part-time job on an unimportant newspaper.

After thirteen years of struggle I relaxed. Not only did I enjoy the act of writing, but also for the first time in my professional life I enjoyed what went with it—meeting new people, planning a skillful interview, following my instincts on a story, and putting it all together. Because the children were no longer the only focus of my day, because playing with them was no longer an obligation but a choice, I again took pleasure in the routine duties of motherhood. My only regret was that it had taken me so long to discover that I was a woman who craved the challenge of work. Without it I felt diminished, half-alive.

The main office of the Genesee Valley Newspapers was a renovated landmark building on the main street of Pittsford. The entire staff was squeezed onto the second floor of this early-nineteenth-century structure, where I eagerly presented myself for my first day of work. Three full-time and three part-time reporters put out five weeklies, and I expected to be given a typewriter and assignment like everyone else. But since Wolfe had failed to inform his managing editor that a new reporter had been hired, there was neither a free typewriter nor an inch of desk space to accommodate me at the horseshoe table around which everyone sat. I was sent up to a cavernous, unoccupied ballroom and for eight hours eyed the drama of wasps mating on the ceiling. As an alternative to Siberia I proposed writing at home where my old Royal portable had been set up on our former kitchen table in an attic room. Like most fugitive housewives, I was initially eager to work in an honest-to-god office with other adults, but I soon realized that laboring within eyesight of Wolfe was an experience I could easily live without. The office seethed with discontent like a ship forever on the verge of mutiny. So I gradually transformed what I had assumed was a temporary arrangment into a permanent one. Like a free-lancer I arranged my own schedule, worked my own hours, thought up a majority of my stories, directed press releases and business calls home, and only dropped into the office to check out my copy, receive approval on my next story, and pick up my minuscule paycheck.

Many journalists, I have since discovered, would rather sweep the streets than work in isolation. But among other self-discoveries was the realization that, by temperament, I was a free-lancer. I preferred the silence of my sanctuary to the chatter of other machines. I disliked taking orders. And I was capable of working to an inner clock. Occasionally, I missed the camaraderie of office life, but within a few months I developed friendships among the staff despite or, perhaps, because of my distance from it. Imperceptibly, too, I developed my craft.

The newspapers' managing editor, Richard Woodworth, recognized my feature-writing talents but often groaned at the length and essaylike tone of my stories. "Here comes part two of the Golden Bowl," he would announce with mock horror as I made my weekly appearance, copy in hand. He was a first-rate newspaperman and put the final touches on my education as a reporter. Although I would never become expert at covering and writing fast-breaking news, under his tutelage I occasionally banged out a piece of readable prose in half an hour. However I wisely absented myself from the frenzy of deadline scenes and considered it a great blessing not to be confronted with those small, suburban stories, like "Clambake Set for Knights of Columbus," for which I had less patience than folding laundry.

The GVN papers were not, as I had hoped, an oasis of liberalism. Politically, Wolfe's views ran the gamut from Rockefeller Republicanism to Goldwater Republicanism, although his editorial rhetoric appeared more progressive than the equally conservative Gannett press. Every newspaper in Rochester, for example, endorsed the Conservative candidacy of James Buckley for the U.S. Senate. Despite the city's technical ties to New York State, it was really an eastern outpost of the Midwest.

Rochester had once been dubbed "Smugtown." Since the 1964 riots and the escalating demands of blacks and Puerto Ricans for better housing, jobs, and a piece of the corporate wealth, Rochester was no longer smug. But it was still pious. For generations the city had been dominated by a small coterie of bankers, lawyers, old-family businessmen, and executives from the largest corporations who sat on each other's boards, ran the Community Chest, the prestigious clubs, the symphony, the university, and set Rochester's non-progressive tone. The postwar rise of Xerox and the huge influx of outside executive talent (often transient) was slowly opening up and liberalizing the community, but if there was an unspoken establishment, Andrew Wolfe was an influential and respected member of it. Although he had come to Rochester as a young reporter, Wolfe was a canny business-man with an appetite for newspaper acquisition and real estate, and his newspapers reflected the concerns of the propertied, white, middle class. In theory, he might support the need for low-income housing, but when it came to a specific project slated for one of his suburban towns, a reason was often found—like unimaginative architecture—to reject it.

Wolfe was only in his late forties, but he dressed like a man in his fifties and bemoaned the civilities of the past like a man in his sixties. He could not tolerate the anger of the disaf-fected. Although he had come to oppose the war in Vietnam —because we weren't winning—he reserved his greatest contempt not for Nixon but for antiwar activists who dis-rupted downtown traffic or a Sunday morning church serv-ice. Women's lib was also anathema. My first week on the job I innocently suggested a local story on the subject. Wolfe shuddered. As one sophisticated person to another he confided that the women's libbers he knew were bored, sub-urban housewives who spawned unhappy marriages and neurotic children. It would be an act of mercy *not* to expose them. I said nothing. Months later, when Gloria Steinem lectured at Monroe Community College, I covered the story as hard news.

Wolfe overworked, underpaid, and undervalued his nonunion, largely female staff while his editorials deplored the loss of old values—decency, politeness, concern for one's fellow man. Few serious reporters could stomach it for very long. There was a constant turnover and a constant supply of bright-eyed hopefuls to replace whoever left.

In fairness, Wolfe's shoestring operation was and is no worse than most. The immensely profitable, Rochester-based Gannett press—today the largest newspaper chain in the country—enjoys an equal reputation for low wages and anti-unionism. Nothing has remained more consistent in our his-tory than the tradition of wealthy, conservative publishers and exploited, liberal reporters. But Wolfe displayed a particular genius for hiring middle-class housewives who were less interested in money than interesting work. They lacked the kind of ambition that is taken for granted in a man, and it was assumed I fit into that mold.

At first I did. I had no thought of going on to something better. I was grateful for the job. Not only could I work it around my family obligations, but also it turned out to be an unmatchable passport into the most interesting segments of the community. Through it I met the kind of people—painters, photographers, dancers, writers, city planners, working women—with whom I had more in common than den mothers. I was not about to rock the boat. Not yet.

Within a few months I was asked to write a weekly column called "The Arts." My managing editor envisaged it as a tony gossip column, wherein it is reported that Mrs. Hubert Hope, Jr., is hosting a benefit for one-armed musicians in her Precipice Drive home. I had other ideas. I saw myself as a critic of the arts and immediately let forth a barrage of opinions on everything from the new TV season to the disasters of urban renewal. I reviewed films (never done since movie theaters did not advertise in a weekly), books, panned road companies charging exorbitant prices for performances that in New York would have been booed off the stage, and urged readers into craft shops and art exhibits no one else bothered to note. I insisted on being taken as seriously by the cultural institutions in the community as my counterparts on the Gannett papers, which meant being notified of press conferences, invited to opening nights, and granted access to visiting celebrities. My new-found aggressiveness paid off. I was deluged with more work than I could possibly handle. I began to pick and choose whom I would see and which galas were worth attending. But more unexpectedly, as can only happen in a small community, my by-line brought me the prestige and power that any journalist seeks and that, in New York, is doled out to very few. Although I was more aware than anyone of the provincial quality of my success, I had to admit I was having a helluva good time.

Jerry, on the other hand, was coasting downhill from his

euphoric high of the previous January. Perhaps it was simply
a delayed case of culture shock. Or perhaps his job, now that
the courtship was over and the honeymoon a dim memory,
was less exciting than he had hoped.

I say perhaps, because I didn't know. And whenever I
probed, sought to discover what was new at the office or what
Jerry was feeling, he became annoyed.

"Everything's fine," he would say. "Stop trying to take my
temperature. When anything exciting happens I'll let you
know."

"But you don't *look* happy," I would persist. "You seem
just as tense, just as moody as you did in New York when the
stock market was falling apart." Then Jerry would accuse me
of not being satisfied with the kind of person he was—essen-
tially brooding and introverted.

Maybe he's right, I would think. Maybe nothing is wrong
except my expectations. A man can't come home with a big
smile and happy step every night of the week. But I sensed
he was let down, disappointed, even bored. Whether in the
job or our life, it was hard to tell.

In the past, New York had entertained us. A stroll through
Riverside Park, down Madison Avenue or around Greenwich
Village; a neighborhood movie followed by a superb but inexpensive meal at a Szechuan restaurant on Upper Broadway
—that was the only way we knew to fill our leisure hours. Our
efforts to transpose that routine to Rochester were ludicrous.
I remember the first time we went to a movie. It was located
in a shopping center miles out of town. About a dozen other
couples turned up for the show. When it was over, we
emerged into a vast, deserted parking lot. Not a store was
open, not even a place to get a cup of coffee. People silently
filed back into their cars, and so did we, more depressed than
when we had left. This was a night out?

But now, between my job, the children, the house, shopping, cooking, entertaining, I had more than enough to keep
me distracted. It was Jerry who sat, as I had sat months
before, staring out the window, unable to rouse himself to
any activity beyond reading a book or the papers. I had a

wealth of suggestions: go back to the piano, the Eastman School of Music is practically at our back door; get involved in politics, the city is crawling with democratic reformers; take an evening course in city planning—anything. But Jerry waved them all aside, saying he was perfectly content doing nothing. He didn't have to fill his every waking hour with activities, like me. He *liked* unwinding after a day at the office. Okay, okay, I said, thinking, he's turning into the dullest man alive.

The first of our New York friends to make the trek northward were Peter and Alessandra Wolf. They arrived to share our first Thanksgiving in Rochester and were openly surprised at what they found. Instead of a depressed wife and exuberant, executive spouse, they recognized that just the reverse was true. I consciously refrained from voicing my suspicion that all was not well, but after effectively monopolizing the conversation with news of my job and the interesting people I had met through it, Peter turned to Jerry and asked, "But what about *you?* Eleanor seems to be going great guns, yet I don't get the same feeling from you."

It was the kind of observation that could only come from an intimate friend. When Jerry had first considered moving, he instinctively turned to Peter for advice, not only because he was a city planner, but also because he was one of those men to whom one could talk, without embarrassment, of the larger meaning and purpose of one's life. Peter had grown up in New Orleans. He understood the benefits and drawbacks of living in a smaller community, and though he had finally settled in New York, there were aspects of his former life he missed, such as the feeling that one's voice can effect change. Most New Yorkers take their powerlessness and anonymity for granted. But Peter pointed out there was usually a dearth of intelligent, sophisticated men in cities like Rochester. Perhaps Jerry would discover he enjoyed sitting on a civic board or getting involved in local politics. Being a big fish in a little pond had its compensations. Jerry had agreed. Yes, the move might open new vistas, apart from the job itself. But now, like a child who has disappointed his parents, he was full of vague excuses.

"I don't know, Peter," he said, slumped in our club chair. "I put in a long day. I'm traveling a great deal. Maybe I'm just not all that ambitious."

The subject was dropped, but through the Wolfs' eyes I couldn't help but see how far I had come in six months, how I had grown and changed, and how unchanged Jerry appeared by contrast. He was still a stranger to the city, a passive onlooker. He barely knew its streets or its shops. Outside of work he had no friends except my friends. I had become his umbilical cord to society. While part of me resented that arrangement, believed it signified a failure on my husband's part, part of me reveled in the triumph of my achievement and delighted in my husband's failure.

Many women who are forced to move because of their husbands' careers suffer a terrible loss of self-esteem. The implication behind the old-fashioned marriage contract becomes the ruling premise: you don't count. You are the penniless, powerless half of a relationship in which the wage earner calls the shots. Normally, this crude fact of life is neither discussed nor explicitly invoked. American middle-class men are subject to the same self-delusory rhetoric as their wives. They think of themselves as partners, not as benevolent dictators. But when it comes to a career opportunity versus the less-definable matter of family stability or the psychological welfare of a wife, men invoke their power with few qualms.

Regardless of what I told myself, I experienced the uprooting as an humiliation. Out of my need to rebalance the power scale in our family I had unconsciously resolved to be so dazzlingly self-reliant that no accusation of dependency, whether on friends or New York, could ever be used against me again. I also hoped, in resuming a career, to earn an equal voice in any future conflict about where we lived. The rapidity with which I found a job, friends, and a recognized role in the community proved I was not a helpless, passive, unadaptable female as everyone, including myself, had assumed. I also believed it proved that, in every way but one, I was superior to my fifty-thousand-dollar-a-year husband.

What I did not understand is that women, caught in a

superior-inferior definition of marriage, are never the win-
ners. They carry the emotions of the victim with them, no
matter how far or fast they rise. But since I was only dimly
aware of what was driving me to assume the persona of
super-woman, I would be unprepared to face the disastrous
consequences of that role. I was convinced, as were the Wolfs
and everyone who knew us, that the worst was behind, the
best yet to come. It was a natural mistake. Outwardly, we had
settled in with a minimum of strain. Our first Thanksgiving
seemed to underscore our good fortune. It was filled with
good talk and parties. We impressed our old friends with the
sophistication and warmth of new ones. But the highlight of
the weekend—for the Wolfs as well as for me—was a tour of
the Stirling Homex factory.

I had driven past the plant a number of times but had
never yet set foot inside. Now I was not only eager to see this
miracle of technology for myself, but also to share first im-
pressions with Peter, who knew more about modular housing
systems than any of us.

The trip in good weather took half an hour. Once past the
suburb of Henrietta, a two-lane road meandered through
undulating farm country where dairy herds and horses now
dotted the landscape, and that in summer shimmered with
crops of wheat, hay, barley, and corn. It was a drive that gave
Jerry great pleasure. He explained what he knew of the re-
gion's history with the same proprietary tones he had once
reserved for the streets and dwellings of New York.

The Homex compound squatted, improbably, beside a
Black Angus farm, on the eastern bank of the Genesee River.
From the outside it was hardly a monument to corporate
elegance, but a hodgepodge of buildings—the new, two-story
executive wing in front, the hangarlike factory behind it, and
to the left, stretching as far as the eye could see, finished
modules wrapped in white Baggies with the striking symbol
of a crane lifting an orange house repeatedly emblazoned
upon the plastic like a ribbon of color running horizontally
around a square box. There was no attempt at fancy landscaping. Trucks, cranes, flat beds, and machinery lay about

the premises behind a metal gate and fence that were always patrolled. It came as a tremendous shock, then, to step into the sumptuous interior of the executive offices. The walls dripped with expensive, modern artwork, among them Picasso and Chagall prints, and a sleek, open staircase wound up to the second floor, which was an ode to Knoll—nothing flashy, just the finest Eames-Saarinen-Breuer furniture money could buy.

Jerry's office, like those of the other attorneys, was efficiently modern but modest. The only exotic touch for a New York boy was the view of open fields where, in the fall, deer and other wildlife could be seen feeding. But the Yanowitch and Stirling brothers' chambers were show-stoppers. Later on, it would be said by a former employee of Homex that, "Every officer had a better office than Joe Wilson's at Xerox." My only basis of comparison was New York, and by New York standards, the roughly fifteen-by-forty-foot rooms were incredibly plush. In addition to private bathrooms (David rated a shower), there were recessed steel-and-rosewood cabinets, bars, the latest electronic business equipment plus a full complement of overstuffed chairs and couches in discreet shades of brown, formally assembled around glass-and-steel coffee tables. Bill Stirling had lined the shelves behind his desk with a collection of pre-Columbian art. Had it not been for the presence of a desk and phone, his room might have been mistaken for a home-entertainment center.

Obviously the Stirlings had spared no expense. It was one of the unwritten rules of their philosophy that the appearance of success bred further success; that to become a corporate giant, one had to pretend the miracle had already taken place. It never seemed to occur to them, as it often did to others, that what was appropriate to, say, the president of Kodak, was inappropriate to the president of a struggling, young company with total assets, as of July 1969, of only $9.1 million. Of course, with Homex's fortunes still rising, and its stock, although down from its high, still holding nicely in a bear market, no one questioned the certainty that within a few years the company would become another Xerox. But because of Jerry's past experience, the lavish setup made me uneasy. It reminded me, unhappily, of the boom-and-bust mentality of his former law associates: if you've got it, flaunt it. I could understand the boost in morale that working in such an atmosphere created, but privately I thought it was too much, too soon.

The rest of the administrative offices were impersonal, undivided large rooms with monotonous rows of gray metal desks. Jerry led us through these deserted caverns, then down a long passageway, lined with hardhats, that connected to the factory where the townhouses were being built.

The modules ran on a single track through the middle of a space the size of several jumbo hangars. On either side of the assembly line, at different work stations, were mountains of raw material—lumber, thick rolls of linoleum, carpeting, piles of kitchen cabinets, toilets, sinks—which were fed into the rooms at appropriate stages. Depending on the number of bedrooms ordered, a house would ultimately be comprised of three or four modules stacked and joined together. Twenty modules could be completed in a day and, according to the prospectus, once they had been trucked to a prepared site, could be readied for occupancy within three hours. Three hours! It took us longer to assemble one of Joshua's Christmas toys.

In fact, to Joshua, each module looked like a life-size dollhouse. He was enchanted with the assembly line and insisted on seeing each cube from its initial stage as a mere wooden shell to its final stage as a completed section of a house. To the adults, the charm of the process was its lack of mystery. Yes, we were in a factory, but what was taking place within it was apprehensible to the least-mechanical mind. Despite all the mumbo jumbo about a revolutionary industrial process, the nails of the house were still hammered by people, the cabinets were installed by people, and the rooms would soon be inhabited by people. We emerged, blinking into the daylight, in a happy mood, delighted to have encountered a rational scheme serving rather than dehumanizing man.

But the tour through plant number one was like a visit to

Sturbridge Village compared to the wonders awaiting us on a separate bit of acreage down the road known as plant number two. There, in all its surprising grace, stood the four-story, steel-and-concrete high rise which, if all went well, was soon to be put into production. It was Homex's secret weapon.

What was extraordinary about the prototype was not its design, but the manner in which it would be erected. Theoretically, it would rise top-floor first. Hydraulic, electronically controlled jacks would lift factory-produced steel-and-concrete modules ten feet off the ground. Then another entire floor would be slipped under the first. Both floors would again be raised, until a building of up to twenty stories would be in place. The system was a genuine breakthrough in high-rise construction. If it worked it would render the slow, dangerous, weather-dependent crane process obsolete. Once mass production was established, it would also mean a far-cheaper product. This was the system that had lit up the eyes of George Romney, and that had received a HUD "Operation Breakthrough" award to build in Kalamazoo and Memphis. The future of Homex rested on its success. With it Homex could compete for office buildings, motels, dormitories, and residential apartments. That was where the big money was to be made.

Visitors to the high rise were first ushered into a small building in front of it. The ostensible purpose of the building was to house the electronic equipment that monitored and controlled the hydraulic jacks. But to insiders it was jokingly known as "the chapel," because its real effect was to provide a setting of worship for the high rise.

Upon entering the room one's eye was immediately drawn to the floor-to-ceiling windows which, like a gargantuan cockpit, offered a 180-degree view of the four-story, terraced building. Below the windows thousands of buttons, dials, knobs, and switches swept around a curved wall, like something out of Houston's Mission Control. Behind this technological stage set rose a carpeted lounge area and amphitheater.

No doubt the buttons and dials could have been set up in a temporary shack. But the Stirlings never wasted a P.R. opportunity. It was easy to imagine the effect on market analysts, government officials, and foreign dignitaries of, first, a chauffeured ride from the airport to Avon during which they were entertained by a film, *The Homex Story,* projected on a small screen in the back seat of the company limousine. Then a tour through plant number one; a "briefing" seated in the *2001* setting of "the chapel"; and finally, the *pièce de résistance,* a tour of the high rise itself.

So spectacular were the model rooms of single efficiencies, dormitories, and apartments for the elderly, that *House and Garden* devoted the cover and four inside pages of its September 1971 issue to this fantasy of "twenty-four-hour living." Postage-stamp space was transformed into high-fashion drama by an inspired mixture of pop graphics, ultra-modern furniture, blazing primary colors, and bold fabrics.

The Wolfs, like so many friends we later took on the same tour, were dazzled. It was as though Henry Ford II had commissioned Peter Max to transform his Edsel into an Aston-Martin.

I still had reservations about the Stirlings' compulsion to project an image of opulence second to none. But despite these reservations I was genuinely excited by the high rise. It was a handsome piece of architecture, light-years ahead of the fake-Tudors and cedar-shingled numbers now in production. And while the interiors were no Habitat, their modernity convinced me the Stirlings knew what they were doing. It seemed churlish to deny their promotional genius, daring, and hustle. Without these qualities Homex would have remained an idea in someone's head. With them, I had to admit, Homex might become a construction giant of the decade.

As we put the Wolfs back on their plane I could not help feeling the weekend had been the happiest landmark in our new life. Everything had conspired to make it a success. The weather had been unusually springlike. We had entertained and been entertained. We had stayed up till all hours sharing intimacies that are only possible between old friends. And the Homex tour had reconfirmed the wisdom of Jerry's move.

I went to bed Sunday evening exhausted, but less resigned and more hopeful about the future than I had been in months. However, in retrospect, the bleakness of winter was foreshadowed by my discovery, Monday morning, that while we had slept, burglars had ransacked the lower floor of our house. I couldn't believe it. Room-sized rugs, tables, lamps, even the turkey carcass had been spirited away by creatures who had lolled about the living room mixing themselves drinks and carving designs on our mantel with a sharp knife.

Hadn't we *left* the jungle? Hadn't we been told this was the safe American heartland? Well, the joke was on us, and in some perverse way, I relished it. I couldn't wait to spread news of the disaster.

Winter 1970–1971

CHAPTER VI

Every city has its obsessions. Like annual parades and natural disasters, they are part of the communal glue, dwindling shared realities between isolated Americans.

We soon discovered Rochester's chief obsession—the weather. Regardless of the season, a good day was an unexpected gift—to be treasured and noted—a bad day, normal. The phrase, "typical Rochester weather," was like a collective groan. Ultimately, I understood why.

At first I dismissed this monomania as another mark of provincialism. *No one had more important things to discuss.* Out-of-towners, I recalled, had often likened New York City's climate to the extremes of the Gobi Desert, yet I had always found it bearable. I was no blue-eyed blonde from Southern California who had never seen gray skies and snow! But what did I know about the traumatic effect of transplanting a human being from home sod to distant turf? Not a thing.

After Thanksgiving no one talked of anything but winter. When was the first "big one" going to hit? What were the odds on what Rochesterians called an "open winter"—meaning no snow? Were those snow-bearing or rain-bearing clouds? What did the *Farmer's Almanac* have to say?

It was an unnerving drum roll. Despite my refusal to panic, I did what I was told: put snow tires on my car, laid in supplies of canned milk and tuna fish, purchased skimobile suits for the children, sheepskin gloves and ski hats for us.

I thought I was ready for anything. That was to prove untrue. For while I was prepared for the 142.7 inches of snow that fell, almost uninterruptedly between December and March, I was unprepared for the almost-total absence of sun, the depression that accompanies life in a twilight zone, and the draftiness of our charming old house. I was always cold. Getting up in the morning was an heroic act. I took to dressing in the steamy bathroom while Jerry showered. My third-floor office was like the outside of an igloo. After an hour of typing I would rush to defrost my fingers in the oven. My wardrobe, geared to overheated Manhattan apartments, was completely inadequate. My mother sent an electric blanket for Christmas.

But far worse than mere physical discomfort was the way winter deep-froze our social lives. We found ourselves almost as alone and isolated as when we first arrived. Rochesterians coped with the winter, it seemed, by leaving town.

The first mass exodus began during the Christmas holidays. Half of our acquaintances went south, where reservations had been religiously booked the year before. The Yanowitch clan took off for Caracas, Venezuela. Joshua's best friend disappeared on a Floridian camping trip with his family. Even my cleaning lady scraped together enough money for a Trailways bus ticket back home to Sanford, Florida.

The rest of our acquaintances skied—in Vail, Aspen, New England, Canada, the Alps. Anywhere the sun shone. A few, like David Stirling, owned ski lodges and Miami Beach condominiums, to which they regularly commuted.

I met Stirling for the first time at one of those obligatory Christmas parties for executives and wives that are the staple of all corporations. Normally a dreary ritual, it turned out to be a gay evening, partly because the liquor flowed, because the men seemed uniquely bound together by the risks and dreams of their mutual adventure, but also because the setting was David Stirling's home. We had been invited into the magic circle of "Hickory Hill," whose private driveways twinkled with white Christmas lights like garlands of diamonds in an enchanted forest.

David's house, as I had been told, was a simple, suburban ranch, custom-built before the first big gusher had made him a millionaire. But that week he had put the final touches on a new wing to his house—a duplex, entertainment room large enough to hold our party and two more like it. The top floor, which turned out to be a balcony, contained the bar. A wrought-iron staircase spiraled down to the lobbylike living room where banks of sofas were squared up before a stone fireplace. David's parents and a contingent of older people remained below. The Homex party, until it was time for a buffet dinner, jammed around the bar. David Stirling, holding a drink he rarely sipped, mingled upstairs with his guests.

From a distance he was startlingly handsome. Movie-star handsome, burnished by that special mixture of sun, success, and moneyed grace that is the hallmark of American celebrities. But up close he exuded little male charm, none of the sexual bravura that in New York would have accompanied his good looks and style. He was a medium-sized man, broad-shouldered and tailored in the latest fashion. His wife, though pretty, seemed dowdy by comparison. I would have said he was Kennedy Irish, with his thin mouth, sharp nose, blue eyes, high forehead, and reddish brown hair curled stylishly over his collar. But there was a Scottish reserve, a dry, armed coolness about him that invited neither laughter nor warmth. He chatted out of duty. I chatted out of curiosity and saw none reflected in his eyes. He came to life only when I complimented him on the new addition to his house, and when he talked about skiing. He was leaving for the Canadian Laurentians the next day.

I was used to hearing about the glories of skiing. Especially from men in their thirties for whom it was frequently a newfound passion. I suspected that in some of them it was less a sport than a drive to stave off middle age, as with many women who, after their childbearing years are over, become more obsessed with their bodies than when they were young.

It was also a test of courage. Harold Yanowitch, who had recently taken up skiing, was reputed to have fantastic guts, for which he was held in awe. My notions of strength and weakness were of a different order. But to speak of skiing's dangers, to express normal fears was, it seemed, only acceptable in women. The wives of these men were frank and funny about their anxieties. If they had finally come to share their husbands' ardor, the reasons seemed subtly different and more persuasive. To me they stressed its virtue as a family activity; how it had added new social and aesthetic dimensions to their lives.

We were repeatedly invited to join our new friends on their various skiing trips, if not abroad, then on nearby slopes where private clubs and public facilities were mushrooming. I was tempted. Although I despised cold weather and considered myself a confirmed coward, it was obvious our New York way of life would not work up here. We would have to change, become more physical, embrace new patterns of living if we were to be happy. But Jerry said, "Absolutely not." Skiing was too expensive. He was an indoors person. He had not the slightest desire to break his leg on some goddamn mountain.

It was more than just a disagreement over skiing. It was the difference between seeing our new life as an opportunity for growth or simply a change of address. It began as a small fissure, then deepened. Not skiing stood for Jerry's maddening passivity, for his refusal to initiate diversions in our life, for not being the kind of husband I wanted.

So we stayed home while everyone else left. We should have pawned the children to get out of town, even for an overnight in New York. But we didn't, and the weekends began to resemble Sartre's *No Exit*. I dreaded the stretches of unbroken time, with no center, no purpose, the children bored, pleading to be played with, Jerry craving solitude, and me growing bitter at how much I was expected to do.

When it was not snowing, the fierce cold that swept down from Canada made the insides of one's nostrils cling together like ice cubes. The two boys were constantly sick, but even when healthy, the treacherous sidewalks and four-foot snow-drifts made it impossible to send them out to play. My periodic attempts to drag us all out of doors frequently ended in disaster. Most memorable was a Sunday in February when the sun miraculously reappeared and the sky sparkled like a brilliant sapphire dome. Jesse, then a year-and-a-half toddler, had been housebound for weeks. I insisted on suiting him up for a twenty-minute family stroll for *The New York Times*. On the way back and for no apparent reason, he began to howl. The next morning a curved, red welt, like the slash of a scimitar, appeared under his chin. It was an affliction the pediatrician assured me was "going around." Frostbite!

I suspect even the happiest of couples would have found their marriage strained. But by then we were not the happiest of couples. We were like mountain climbers who, six months before, had packed bags for the same expedition and now were grimly headed in different directions. The rope that bound us, that should have been our lifeline, had become a hangman's noose.

I cannot pinpoint when I knew we were in serious trouble. The process of disaffection was gradual. At first I blamed it on the abrupt external changes in our life. Then on my increasing militancy as a feminist. The added responsibilities of a job, an enormous house, two growing and often clashing boys, made me more dissatisfied with the distribution of family burdens. But these only partially explained the downward spin in which we found ourselves. What was also true was that Jerry had changed, for the worse, and I did not know why. It was months before I figured out it was his job and months later before he allowed himself to agree. Until then I assumed that like others in my generation I was struggling to liberate myself from long-held assumptions about the division of labor within a marriage and discovering the depth of my husband's hostility toward change.

Nineteen seventy was not a very good year for the American marriage. It was the year the feminist movement swept through middle-class America like a runaway train. It was the

year a minority revolt became a national revolution. It was
the year women's liberation moved from the woman's page
to the front page. One had only to live outside New York to
appreciate the media's power, its crucial role in spreading
and legitimizing the conflagration. Kate Millett appeared on
the cover of *Time.* Germaine Greer on the cover of *Life.*
Gloria Steinem's face, figure, opinions, and lifestyle became
as ubiquitous as Jacqueline Kennedy's. The homely image of
Betty Friedan was suddenly replaced by multiple images of
snappy, sexy women. Feminism, in its latest reincarnation,
became chic. Like all fashionable movements, it inspired
countermovements. Midge Decter denounced its theories in
the intellectual pages of *Commentary,* others denounced its
goals. Although it was impossible to predict whether the
movement would go the way of spurious fashion or seriously
alter the mainstream of American thought, the shattered
debris of families lay everywhere. Women, high on freedom,
had severed the umbilical cord that was supposed to exist—
only for them—between sex and love. Tensions between husbands and wives, formerly hidden, now flared openly. Everywhere one turned there were articles on divorced, sepa-
rated, communal, lesbian, and runaway wives. They were no
longer fringe freaks but, it seemed, a new breed of heroine,
the vanguard of an insurrection that was about to overtake
us all. Staying married became more difficult than usual.

Since the rebirth of my marriage I had been rather smug
about its enlightened foundation. Jerry, raised to think of
women primarily as mothers and wives, now supported my
desire to work. He was not threatened by an independent
wife. Publicly, we were a united front for equal pay, equality
of opportunity, and equality of ambition.

I, of course, considered myself a woman's libber from way
back. I further believed any intelligent woman who had
faced job discrimination could not help but align herself with
feminism. Yet, for various reasons, I had felt it was no longer
my battle. I was delighted a majority of women were coming
round to what, in my time, had been a minority point of view.
Let them become the book and magazine editors I had once

aspired to be. Let waves of female doctors and lawyers descend upon the land. But for me the rules had changed in midstream. I was already married with two children. I had already narrowed my career options, and whatever changes lay ahead would be within the framework of an established marriage and conventional lifestyle.

I had avoided feminist literature, telling myself, why bother *reading* what I had lived. But that was, I later realized, a rationalization. The truth was I could not handle the profound rage that churned beneath my apparent acceptance of the past. When I read about other women's amputated lives—jobs lost, promotions denied—I relived my own. Whenever my eyes unavoidably strayed across an article on discrimination in book publishing or a sit-in at the editorial offices of the *Ladies' Home Journal,* I became so angry at men, at the systematic oppression of women that had humiliated us for so many years that, like a POW screening films of his captivity, the violence of my emotions was literally unbearable.

One day while I was still living in New York, I tried reading *The Feminine Mystique.* Two relatively innocuous phrases on page thirteen stopped me cold. Friedan wrote about her generation, "Girls would not study physics: it was 'unfeminine.' A girl refused a science fellowship at Johns Hopkins to take a job in a real-estate office."

Suddenly, I remembered a fellowship *I* had turned down with the CARE organization for a summer secretarial job. I had completely forgotten the incident; never thought twice about the choice. But the chilling realization swept through me that it had not been freely taken. Jerry thought the job a waste of time because it was unsalaried. My history teachers emphasized the unlikelihood of a woman achieving an executive position in such an organization. Pressures had been brought to bear that had less to do with me than with a male view of "acceptable" female roles. So that summer I had opted for a practical, dead-end job. Eventually, I had switched my allegiance from history to English. At the time I believed it a simple matter of personal preference. But

wasn't it also true that at Smith and Barnard, male professors
were historians and women English professors? Hadn't I, like
a Pavlovian dog, responded to years of unconscious program-
ing? Women went into the arts. Into literature. That was
"feminine."

I stared at that page for a long time, reliving a turning
point in my life I had never realized *was* a turning point.
How many others had there been? How many times had I
been nudged in a "feminine" direction? How many impulses
and talents had been subtly proscribed?

I closed the book. The anger it aroused frightened me, and
I seemed incapable of a detached response. Later on, my
other women friends would admit to identical feelings.
Rather than torture ourselves, rather than encourage the
bitterness and rage that threatened to turn us against our
husbands, our present lives, and the compromises of the past,
we stayed away from all those feminist books that were radi-
calizing a younger generation.

But with the move to Rochester my situation changed. To
begin with, the process of making new friends required that
I offer and redefine my identity. In New York everyone understood where my sympathies lay. There was no need to
explain why I was a feminist or what the movement was
about. In Rochester it was impossible to remain silent and
still regard oneself, even minimally, a supporter of the movement. I felt like a nonpracticing Jew in a Christian world who
must suddenly make a point of her religion. I also found
myself, confronted by uninformed women, under a compulsion to shake them up, to make them think and, inevitably,
to proselytize.

Then too, once I resumed my career, I was automatically
categorized "a woman's libber." My very presence at a suburban dinner party provoked controversy. Husbands baited
me. Wives expected me to defend the gospel. The role of
spokeswoman was thrust upon me and I began to enjoy it.

Gradually, as I again moved among businessmen, as I again
observed the unconscious biases still rampant, and as I met
other working women in Rochester publicly committed to

changing the system, I found myself becoming more of an activist.

I had never been a joiner. Perhaps because, when I grew up, committeewomen represented what I never wanted to be, I carried within me an irrational bias against groups, from the Junior League to the League of Women Voters. But in 1970 I overcame my reluctance to get involved and extended myself in small but, to me, significant ways.

My first public act of solidarity with the women's movement was unpremeditated. I happened to be in New York City on the day a nationwide march had been planned to commemorate the fiftieth anniversary of the adoption of the woman's suffrage amendment. I was aware of the demonstration that was scheduled to move down Fifth Avenue in the late afternoon and eagerly rushed to Fifty-ninth Street to witness it. Confronted with the spectacle of twenty thousand women of all ages shouting, laughing, milling about in happy anticipation of the surge southward toward Forty-second Street, I could not remain on the sidelines. I felt, as I never had before, that these were my sisters, that this was my revolution. I ducked under the police barricades and, like a homosexual who has decided to "come out," crossed some invisible barrier in my own mind.

I returned to Rochester with a "Women's Liberation" button I wore everywhere, a bumper sticker with a Day-glo symbol of the movement, and a "Women Unite" shopping bag, which I hung on the doorknob of my bedroom closet and was the first object I saw every morning when I opened my eyes.

The march took place in August. In early fall I received a phone call from a friend, a woman city-planner who had recently moved to Rochester from New York, asking me to sit in at a male-only public dining room at the local Treadway Inn. A businesswoman had been refused service. She had begun a legal suit but, in the meantime, waves of mixed couples were being asked to disrupt the lunch hour. We had no plans to go to jail or to be dragged out on our backs, merely to embarrass and harass the restaurant's management and, hopefully, arouse a certain amount of sympathy from the diners. To our surprise, as we were hustled from the room, the men who had averted their eyes throughout our little drama, cheered our eviction. I was more incensed by this male-locker-room mentality than the policy of discrimination itself. I talked about the experience constantly, fired off angry follow-up letters, and spent a depressing evening listening to city councilmen ridicule our efforts to pass a local desegregation ordinance.

Through this incident I became aware of the numerous feminist groups that were becoming increasingly active in Rochester and encountered women as committed to the movement as any I had met in New York. It was exhilarating to participate, with hundreds of other women, in an all-day Rochester conference on "The Working Woman." In addition to workshops and a tough speech by Caroline Bird, posters, buttons, and books were on sale. I bought the books and began to read, almost single-mindedly, about house husbands, part-time work options for men and women, day-care centers, the abortion issue—subjects I knew very little about.

The intensity of my involvement was not unrelated to the fact that I was now trying to juggle the roles of wife, mother, and career woman. It was an exhausting and endless effort. The more I read the more sensitive I became to the gross inequities within my house. Jerry, it turned out, was a liberated husband in theory only. I had been deluding myself about the way our marriage worked.

When I had emerged in 1969 from four years of maternity clothes, nestbuilding, and a total absorption in schedules, toilet training, nursery schools, apartment decorating, and presiding over Julia Child extravaganzas, the world had radically changed. It was as though I had been in hibernation. I awoke to find myself a dowdy representative of the fifties in the hedonistic youth-culture of the sixties. I had never smoked pot. My clothes were out of date. I was still wearing a bra, owned not one mini-skirt or pair of bell-bottoms, and possessed a drawerful of girdles and garter belts. The women's movement and the peace movement were like twin specters haunting my friends, and now I was ready to catch up. I loved my boys, but was delighted my pregnancy days were over. I gave away my maternity clothes and went on the pill. I was thirty-one years old, and the time had come to plan for my future.

I also began to make serious noises about Jerry's attitude around the house. I had not minded his conventional, all-thumbs awkwardness around the first born whom I only reluctantly entrusted to others. But I was less misty-eyed with two children, more harassed and eager for time off. Discontent bubbled up. We quarreled more over park-sitting duties, or Jerry's obligation to baby-sit while I shopped on a Saturday. But I thought these part of the normal adjustment to a growing family. And when our nerves were particularly strained, there were groups of friends to call and two sets of grandparents to give us both a day off.

Then the move superseded all problems. I had no choice, when Jerry commuted to Avon, but to take over the children. Jesse was less than a year; Joshua almost five. The weekdays without Jerry were long and often boring. I took to sewing and playing rock music and dancing for hours with Joshua in the dining room almost as a way of filling up the silence. I believed this arrangement a temporary state of affairs, but it had its insidious repercussions.

Jerry became used to *visiting* the family rather than partaking of it. I became used to running it. During the last weekends we spent in New York, I was like a tour guide. I would greet Jerry at the door on Friday night with a schedule all worked out. He had only to relax and enjoy the social sights. Then, when we moved, the pattern persisted, as though it were a natural part of our new life.

I had not quite realized the extent of this imbalance until my sister came to visit one winter weekend. Seven years younger, unmarried, an instructor of philosophy at the University of Pittsburgh, she had driven up with her latest boyfriend in tow. We had not been close for many years. I had married while she was in junior high school. During my early marital crises she was too young to confide in. During her graduate school years, when she really became an adult, we were three thousand miles apart. We had grown up in different eras, had taken separate paths as women, which made us ill at ease and defensive in front of one another.

The weekend was to prove a turning point in our relationship. It was such a disaster it forced us to confront our hostility and work at becoming friends again. But at the time she believed I disapproved of her life. She detected in me pressures on her to conform, to marry, to settle down. And I was certain she saw me as the apotheosis of convention—relentlessly middle class and square.

It was true I had little idea what her life was like and fell into old formulas for finding out. "Are you serious about someone?" I would gingerly inquire. Or, "What happens when you finish your Ph.D?" It was clear she resented such questions, mistook them to mean, "When are you going to marry and become a normal woman like me?" So she flung back replies calculated to exacerbate our differences. "I've just gotten to the point," she boasted, "where I won't make a bed for a man. Or cook dinner. If he doesn't like it, he can leave."

I had mixed emotions about her independence. My bourgeois instincts welled up. "But don't you think, I mean living with a man, you have to do *something?*"

"Nope," she replied, and I knew she meant it, couldn't care less how her apartment looked, whether the dishes piled up or her odd living habits—sleeping late and often going to bed at three in the morning—fit in with the man of the moment. It had taken her twenty-six years to find her own rhythms, to separate images of what society said she should be from what was natural for her to be. Begrudgingly I admired that strength, because it was precisely what I had never allowed myself.

The differences between us were partly feminist, partly matters of temperament. Although as children of the same parents our anxieties and ambitions were similar, the way we worked them out were not. I couldn't stand clutter. Pamela was indifferent to it. I was a plodder, worked steadily, left

nothing to the last moment. Pamela had the flair of the exceptionally gifted, worked best under pressure and only at
the last moment. Even as a child she had been addicted to
the Late, Late Show. Now she was a confirmed night person
who came fully awake when I was ready for my afternoon
nap. I hadn't realized how rigid I had become, until she
arrived.

Saturday morning Pamela dutifully dragged herself down
to breakfast. I had already made the beds, dressed, diapered
the baby, emptied the dishwasher, set the table, and prepared breakfast. I almost flinched when this disheveled,
shoeless, semicomatose creature wandered in. I prided myself on being organized, efficient, a step ahead of everyone
else, but it drained me, leached me of the slightest sympathy
for lesser mortals. I didn't want to be the family fascist without whom the trains would never run on time, but seeing
myself through Pamela's eyes, I understood that was what I
had become. Both a tyrant and a slave. I saw myself jump up
and down to serve coffee, toast, cereal, milk; saw myself clean
up the dishes, leap to the baby in the highchair when he
cried, rush to change his diaper—a speeded-up puppet nerv-
ously twitching as the other drowsy adults remained motion-
less. Jerry, as usual, was oblivious to the fact that I was doing
everything and he nothing. But Pamela noticed. Her eyes
narrowed. She watched, and I could almost hear her thinking, "Jesus Christ, marriage is worse than I thought!"

I was ashamed of my chains and hated her for forcing me
to notice them. How could I pretend this was a remotely
liberated marriage? It was altogether different from being
admired by my mother or other women for my efficiency. "A
job, two children, a big house, how do you do it all?"

"It's not so difficult," I would say, with that detestable false
modesty that veiled an overweening pride. Because of my
superior energy, talent, and will, I would privately think. But
in front of my sister I thought, because I'm a fool, because
I've allowed myself to believe that being a superwoman will
bring me love and respect. All it really brings is resentment
in me and indifference in my husband.

For the rest of the weekend I perpetuated the charade of

happy housewife in an altered state of mind. I perceived its price as I never had before: my anger in the kitchen as I fed the children and Jerry chatted in the living room. The fury I felt when Jerry informed me Jesse had moved his bowels and would *I* please change his diaper. Jerry's unawareness of how my workload had tripled suddenly became intolerable. Oh yes, intellectually he was still an ally. He wouldn't dream of calling the restaurant sit-in "trivial," as so many other men we knew did. And he shook his head sadly when I pointed out how, at a Xerox party for the press, a hostess had welcomed *him,* and a lecherous male had sidled up and jocularly said, "Don't tell me *you're* a reporter!"

But whenever my demands affected him personally, whenever I suggested he make a bed, clear a dish, or change a diaper, he bridled. Frequently that winter I would come home from an hour of food shopping on a Saturday to find the breakfast dishes uncleared, Joshua watching cartoons still in his pajamas, the baby soaked with urine, and Jerry buried in *The New Yorker.*

"My God, couldn't you even change the kid's diaper?" I would hiss.

"Is Jesse wet?" Jerry would innocently reply, making not the slightest move to remedy the situation.

"Yes, he's wet, you bastard, and cold. Now change him while I put away the groceries."

"But you know I always prick my fingers. I'm no good at it. Now that you're back, you do it."

"Go to hell," I would reply, and for me, the day was ruined.

After my sister left, and as the winter deepened, my attitude around the house underwent a profound change. Tasks that I had previously done without thinking, I either refused to do or carried out with intense bitterness. Like a miser I measured what I would and would not give. If I made breakfast, then let Jerry clean it up. If he wanted to go to a movie, then let him make ten phone calls to find a baby-sitter. If he wanted the bed made, let *him* make it. I would no longer be a servant in my house.

But that is not a marriage. It is guerrilla warfare—every

place a battle ground, each hour of the day a deadly contest of will with no time off and no neutral zone.

Whenever I tried to establish rules, whenever I suggested we sit down and draw up a list of shared obligations, Jerry refused.

"I will not operate on a schedule. I will not be told when I can go out and when I can stay in, when I have to make breakfast and when I don't. I can't stand this tit for tat routine. It's like being in the army. Now get off my back."

Part of me understood that, despite my aggravated feminism, our quarrels over "chores" were as much a symptom of our deteriorating marriage as a cause. I knew from past experience that when Jerry and I were happy with one another, I did not pounce on this or that activity as a symbol of my exploitation. I gave freely, knowing that emotionally I was being given to in return. Gratitude and affection would have made the inequities bearable. They would not have altered patterns that needed alteration, but they would have established a mood of love, without which meaningful change could not flourish.

In the past, when Jerry was at peace with himself, when he was happy at work and confident about the future, it was evident in his generosity, patience, and thoughtfulness at home.

When we moved to Rochester I believed an unwritten but binding bargain had been struck. In return for my giving up New York, Jerry would give more of himself to me and the family. The only reason this terrible upheaval had made any emotional sense for me was the expectation of a joyful household. Now I felt bitterly betrayed. All Jerry's talk about coming home early, about family Sundays around a fire, about ice-skating together and building snowmen had been sucker's bait. I had been duped. If anything, Jerry was more withdrawn, distracted, and remote than ever. The children grated on his nerves. He grew sentimental about them only when they were in bed. I was too demanding. He complimented me only in front of others. But in private neither I nor the children gave him any discernible pleasure. Nothing, in fact, pleased him except being left alone. So during that first winter, when the newness of the move had worn off, when the weather closed in, our new friends vanished, and the irritations of family living that had begun to surface in New York now erupted in full force, I began to wonder whether money or job pressures or where we lived had much to do with our problems. Theoretically, Jerry had everything he ever wanted, but it had not sweetened his disposition or changed his attitude. Perhaps we were simply incompatible in the familiar way of two people whose expectations of themselves and their marriage are radically different.

In some respects it was as though I had opened a door and found myself gazing straight into the hell of ten years before. Bitterness, coldness, and the estrangement that transcends individual quarrels, had returned. All those painfully learned lessons about keeping doors of communication open, about discussing without attacking, had been lost. We seemed to be living separate lives. There were perfunctory exchanges of news, but Jerry's lack of responsiveness made me less and less eager to fill him in on my day.

We rarely fought in front of the children and were very good—old hands, you might say—at keeping up a front at an infrequent party. What was most destructive was invisible—our silence. No one suspected that this bright, young, successful couple who appeared to have everything, had less and less each day. Even I sometimes wondered if things were as bad as I imagined. For the most part, we were exceedingly civil, and occasionally, when we got drunk at home, we joked and pretended everything was fine. But the next morning we would quarrel over who was to get out of bed first or whose turn it was to drive Joshua to a Saturday morning photography class. I would become angry; Jerry would retreat into martyred silence, and the destructive pattern would begin all over again.

The only passion I seemed capable of sustaining was anger. I was angry all the time. I refused to accept the occasional flicker of affection or helpful gesture as anything more than a temporary bribe to purchase my silence. Like royalty, Jerry might stoop to pick up a toy or throw his arms around me an hour before suggesting we make love. But I no longer wanted to make love. I was incapable of separating sexual intimacy from the full range of other intimacies that are the essence of marriage. When Jerry stopped touching me except as a direct prelude to sex, when he balked at the slightest imposition of the family on his time, I simply turned to stone.

I was afraid to say what I felt because I felt that everything was wrong; the marriage was failing and it was my husband's fault. Outside of my work, I was terribly unhappy. I still missed New York, but the absence of cosmopolitan amenities —a first-rate bookstore, restaurant, or theater—seemed less significant than the absence of the city itself. The small cravings of my first months of exile had been replaced by a larger craving for nourishment that could not be filled by pastrami sandwiches and cheesecake. In New York a trip to the supermarket had been an adventure. The city, in all its variety, heightened one's perceptions, reawakened one's senses, and stretched one's mind. In Rochester a shopping expedition was a nonevent. Although on one level my life was more active than it had been in New York, I still felt as though deep within me a battery that had once been charged was dead. The city was a negative space through which I moved.

I was hungry, too, for literary conversation and a circle of good friends rather than good acquaintances. I missed the relative simplicity of running an apartment as opposed to our money-sucking, toy-strewn house. But above all I missed the closeness that Jerry and I had achieved before the move. Despite my anxieties about leaving the city, Jerry's happiness and expectations for the future had been infectious. He bubbled with news, with plans and confidence, and we both understood that a curtain was about to be raised on one of the great dramas of our life. But now Jerry was like a man for whom the great drama of life was over. He had flared like a candle, drawn me into his glow, and then settled into a dark that was even gloomier for having once been bright. He rarely talked, either about the company, his work, or the people at work whose personalities, at first, had fascinated him as though they were characters in a Dickens novel. When I talked about my growing ambitions at the paper, Jerry no longer speculated about his future. He was a closed box and gradually I lost interest in communicating with it.

Jerry's silence about his work made me suspect that his job had become a disappointment. Like most wives, denied a direct view of my husband's daily life, I relied on my intuition to fill in the empty picture. And what I sensed was that Jerry was bored, was not being given enough work or responsibilities. During the stock offering I knew, almost hour by hour, what he was doing, what aspect of the prospectus he was working on, whom he was seeing, and what problems still lay ahead. But since then, I had no clear idea of what he did every day. I knew that Reuben Davis had become Harold Yanowitch's administrative assistant. I knew that Tommy SantaLucia was in charge of specific building projects in Buffalo and Erie. But Jerry seemed to have no broad area of responsibility. Occasionally he would mention an employment agreement he had drawn up or a minor local lawsuit. But he had not come to Stirling Homex for that. Was Jerry, because of personality conflicts or because Harold had hired more lawyers than he needed, outside the company's mainstream activities? Was he superfluous and beginning to suspect he had made a career mistake?

I remembered once, when I was about ten, asking my mother what my father did. He was that vague thing, a consultant, and I could never figure out what it meant. My mother replied, with a small laugh, that she wasn't always sure herself, that he wrote reports and advised people, but I was not to worry, he made a good living and was respected by his clients. I had thought, how strange that a wife doesn't know what her husband does, and secretly vowed it would be different with me. Now I felt my life had come full circle. Just like my mother I knew so little, and because Jerry resented being asked what was new at the office, I was growing less informed every day. And just like my mother, I seemed to have married a man who could not leave the office at a normal hour, who rarely played with his children, and hid behind a newspaper or book until late at night. If my suspicions about Jerry's lack of serious work were correct, why was he coming home later and later? Even worse, he was making fewer excuses about his erratic schedule, forcing me to pry and probe like a grand inquisitor.

"When will you be home tonight?" I would inquire, trying to sound casual, at breakfast.

"I'm not sure. I may have to work late."

"Well, would you call and let me know?"

"I can't always get out of a meeting and call."

"Why the hell not?"

"Because it's awkward. Besides, when I do call you sound so frosty, it hardly seems worth the effort. You resent my working late, period."

"That's not true," I would protest. "What I resent is not knowing when you'll come sailing through that door. What I resent is not being able to tell the children whether you'll be home in time to put them to bed or not. If you were in my place for a week, if you knew how difficult those hours between five and seven are, you'd be sympathetic to my needs. I'm not making unreasonable demands. My life is as circumscribed as yours. It's not fair turning me into a nag."

When a woman has made enormous sacrifices for her marriage and then feels herself treated like a hired hand, no number of sessions with Masters and Johnson can make her want to make love. We were only going through the motions of cohabitation, and even the motions were getting more difficult for me. But my feelings were different from what they had been ten years before. I was not confused or frightened. I was asking Jerry to behave like a normal husband. If he was, by temperament or inclination, incapable of fulfilling that role, then I would have to seriously consider ending the marriage. Divorce no longer conjured up unnamable terrors. I had no illusions about the difficulties of raising two boys by myself, but I knew I could if I had to. I could go back to New York, reclaim our sublet apartment, find a job, and begin again. The times were with me. Networks of sympathy and support existed between women that had not existed ten years before. And my confidence, because of what I had learned about myself through the move, was at an all-time high. I would not put up with this situation forever. Although I didn't want one, I thought about the possibility of divorce continually.

Spring–Summer 1971

CHAPTER VII

It is commonly assumed that corporations, like women, spend inordinate amounts of time and money on making up their public face, and that the average investor, despite the information that can be gleaned from annual reports, press releases, and prospectuses, has as much chance of seeing the whole truth as a boy out on his first date.

A parallel assumption, less true, is that within the privacy of the executive suite, candor prevails; there is something called "inside information," which can be manipulated by company executives to their advantage. Like most conspiracy theories, a vision of top management seated around a conference table plotting denies a more complex reality. First, that within board rooms, some executives are more equal than others. Second, that "inside information" may be a double-edged sword: it can mislead the insider as well as anyone else. In fact many members of so-called top management possess, to an astonishing degree, tunnel vision and are frequently the last to perceive what is going on.

Despite my husband's impressive titles and, to the outside world, apparent stature within the company, it became clear to me by late February, when Jerry began hearing rumors of a second stock offering, that he was rarely consulted and only intermittently informed of Homex's important plans. It was too small an organization not to notice the numbers of invest-

ment brokers streaming up to Avon but when Jerry asked
Yanowitch what was up, the typically veiled response was,
"We're seeing people from New York."

I was appalled by this personal rebuff, especially since
Jerry had been hired for his securities background, but Jerry
seemed only mildly rankled. No one at Stirling Homex, with
the exception of Harold Yanowitch, had any illusions about
being fully privy to inside information. Jerry was used to
being kept in the dark about many aspects of company business, even accepted it as a condition of employment. His first
week on the job Yanowitch had bluntly laid out the rules:
Homex ran on a "need to know" basis—a military term that
meant executives were given as much information as needed
to carry out a specific assignment and no more. It also meant
Jerry was never to discuss his work with anyone else, nor
others their work with him. If, for example, he required a
sales figure for the first draft of a prospectus, he would have
to clear his request through Harold who, in turn, cleared it
through David. David Stirling ran the show. He alone understood the big picture. Everything went up to the top and
came down from the top.

The explanation given for this interoffice secrecy was the
sensitive nature of the modular-housing business. Homex,
with its new patents and innovative manufacturing proc-
esses, was vulnerable to industrial espionage. Also, because
the company was continually engaged in complex negotiations with municipal and federal agencies, partial or premature disclosure of facts might prove damaging.

Of course a healthy disparity between theory and practice
existed. While officially each man was to stick to his narrow
slot and keep his mouth shut, Jerry and his colleagues were
in and out of each other's offices and, at lunch or over a drink,
discussing company business.

But Harold's directive had its subtle effect. At work or
during our infrequent social evenings with Jerry's fellow attorneys, no one completely let down his guard. It was as if
curtains would fall in midconversation. Eyes shifted, drinks
were refreshed, and the subject awkwardly moved to safer

ground. But I thought that the nature of all corporate life.

More distressing were the ways in which Harold's obsession with secrecy and lines of authority affected me. I was
convinced Jerry's reluctance to talk freely about his work at
home partially stemmed from Harold's constraints. When
Jerry occasionally passed on a bit of office gossip or news, it
was with the unfailing reminder to keep it strictly to myself.
Inwardly I was indignant. But admittedly, though I had
never yet breached a confidence, the situation in which I
found myself was unprecedented. In New York our social life
and Jerry's professional life were absolutely separate. But in
Rochester, especially during our first months, my two closest
friends were the boss's wife, Joan Yanowitch, and Marge
Rosen, whose husband was Homex's director of planning for
three years before he quit. Once I resumed work our social
circle broadened and my almost-daily communication with
Joan ceased, but by then many of Harold and Joan's intimate
friends had become *our* intimate friends. I had no intention
of short-circuiting those friendships, and yet maintaining and
deepening them required extraordinary tact and self-control. The same women who six months before seemed so
indifferent to the women's movement were turning toward
me like tender shoots toward the sun. They trusted me and
talked freely about growing career ambitions and unresolved
conflicts between work and family. They admired me and
sought my advice. I wished to be equally frank about my
emotional life, but because it was so bound up with Jerry's,
and because I feared the slightest criticism of my husband
might find its way back to Harold and Joan, I could not open
up. I could not express to Marge my suspicions that Jerry was
bored and underworked at Homex, and that his job dissatis-
factions were poisoning our marriage. And I certainly could
not express my progressive disenchantment with Harold,
whom our mutual friends regarded with awe.

Privately, the more I saw of him the less I found to admire.
But above all I disliked what others found most admirable—
his uncritical commitment to David Stirling and obsessive
dedication to Stirling Homex. He believed, as he once told

Jerry, "in suppressing one's ego for the greater good of the company." He viewed conflict as disloyalty.

But I kept these thoughts to myself. In the beginning they were shared by no one, least of all my husband who admired Harold's single-mindedness and self-control. In fact, Jerry expressed few complaints at the way the company was run. It was, after all, his first inside view of a corporation. He was eager to become a successful member of the management team. Homex was a raging success, and Jerry had been around businessmen long enough to know that confidentiality and a slight paranoia about competitors were a normal state of affairs.

But by the spring of 1971 it became apparent, even to my husband, that the atmosphere within the company had changed. Secrecy and suspicion increased and plant security, which had always been tight, seemed to double. Entering the premises was like being admitted to a military installation. Locked gates swung open when identification cards were flashed. Visitors to the assembly line were screened. Uniformed guards and a plain-clothes force patrolled the grounds. There were rumors of antiunion incidents and guards protecting truckers. But even executives were being more closely watched. New rules were invoked: documents could not be taken from one building to another without forms being filled out in the presence of guards, and no one was allowed to remove from the premises, without special approval, architectural or engineering plans. To men like Richard Rosen who had spent years at other housing companies, such white-collar policing was outrageous and totally baffling.

Even more bizarre in my view was the choice of an ex-federal agent to head up security. It was like bringing in a SAM II rocket to guard a dog kennel. Jerry assured me there was nothing sinister about his presence. Federal agents frequently went into civilian work for better pay. Besides, the man in question was a down-to-earth guy who bore no resemblance to my stereotyped image of a tough cop.

I met him at the Homex Christmas party. He reminded me

of a young Frank Sinatra—small, wiry, with an extremely pretty wife. He liked Jerry and went out of his way to ingratiate himself with me. Although he presented himself as a fun-loving regular guy, his years in security work had left him with a distorted view of the world. Everyone, he confided after a few drinks, had something to hide. Only the innocent believed otherwise. Since I came from the big city he assumed I shared his cynicism. I did not and in a friendly way disagreed.

One day, Jerry came home with the astounding rumor that the entire company—phones, washrooms, private offices— had been bugged. They flatly denied it; among other things, the cost of such massive surveillance would be prohibitive. I was unconvinced. From what I had seen, the Stirlings had no inhibitions about spending money. But what the rumor confirmed was that everyone, including my husband, believed the Stirlings capable of such behavior. In light of what eventually transpired, it was probably false, but the paranoid atmosphere it reflected was real enough.

At first Jerry and I were equally agitated by the news. But within a few days Jerry believed the denial. He could not allow himself to take such gossip seriously, and yet he casually suggested we say nothing of importance over the phone from then on. When I pointed out, with some asperity, we rarely talked by phone anymore, Jerry lightly retorted, "Just as well, isn't it?" and went upstairs to change.

I sat in the living room mulling over this latest revelation. Up until then I had been only vaguely disturbed by the company scene—Harold's cult of secrecy, the guards, Jerry's exclusion from corporate policies, and what I had come to think of as David Stirling's benevolent dictatorship. But now all these negative feelings seemed less the neurotic imaginings of an unhappy, uprooted wife than alarmingly accurate. Despite Homex's reputation in Rochester as a progressive company (which probably had more to do with its high salaries and visible black executives), it sounded more like an army, with David Stirling the chief of staff and Harold his five-star general. All those so-called executives were spear carriers for David and, like many men credited with genius and the Midas touch, it was believed the warrior could do no wrong. But what was the meaning of career success if it meant "suppressing one's ego" and, in my husband's case, not being trusted to participate in policy decisions directly related to his area of expertise? What happened to men who only found themselves carrying out orders? They swallowed their pride and displaced their anger in exchange for a fat check every week. They brooded and withdrew into themselves, and expected their wives to operate under the same rules of blind loyalty. Don't ask too many questions. Keep your mouth shut. Keep your unrealistic moral scruples to yourself. Do your housewifely chores. Don't make unreasonable demands and in return you will be taken care of. The husband as benevolent dictator.

Ironically, just as Jerry was beginning to admit David's lack of candor with his staff was a growing company problem, he refused to admit our lack of candor was a growing marital problem. He persisted in attributing our quarrels to my heightened feminism rather than to his increased irritability with and indifference to the two-way obligations of marriage. My feminist "phase" would pass just as Homex's administration growing pains would pass. Sooner or later David would realize he could no longer run the company like a family store. And when, I wondered, would Jerry realize he could no longer play the Victorian paterfamilias?

Throughout that sodden, endless spring we both, for different reasons, felt ourselves undervalued and depressed. I was convinced Jerry's passivity at home stemmed from his frustrations at work and from his dimly perceived but constantly denied awareness that Homex was beginning to flounder. I felt like a detective with a strong hunch who cannot prove his theory of the villain. But little by little, without knowing it, Jerry began to provide the corroborating facts.

When it came to the frustrations of *other* executives, he was less inhibited about discussing them with me. So it was Jerry who revealed the bitter complaints of various salesmen and planners. Projects were running into trouble because of a lack of teamwork. David Stirling did not understand what administrative cooperation was all about. He never held conferences; he never sought advice. He simply made off-the-cuff decisions—whether to bid or not to bid on a housing contract—and then expected his technical staff to figure out the details.

"Sounds rather amateurish," I would venture. Jerry would shake his head and shrug, as though to say, "Don't ask me, I'm just a civilian." Sometimes he would speculate whether the whole notion of business competence wasn't as much of a fraud as the myth of efficient armies. If Homex, with all its mistakes, was making a profit, what on earth were other companies like?

Then, increasingly, Jerry began to brood about the temper of the times. Social forces were at work beyond Homex's control. Racism was taking the form of community opposition to low-income housing. It was much harder to obtain sites and zoning variances for subsidized housing. Fewer sales were being consummated; projects were stalled throughout the northeast, and even those that got through were taking more time and money to launch. Everyone was less optimistic. Tommy SantaLucia had even decided not to furnish his expensive house in Pittsford until he was absolutely convinced Homex would survive. The SantaLucias' empty rooms became a wry joke among the four of us. "I'd love to invite you to dinner," Dee would confess, "but Tommy won't let me buy a dining room table."

Finally, it was Jerry who brought home bad news of another sort Richard Karkow, the executive vice-president and treasurer of the company, had just quit.

Karkow was one of the few operating officers who had come to the company with impressive credentials and years of business experience. Like many others, he had traded job security for the once-in-a-lifetime opportunity of becoming a millionaire. He was Homex's fourth-highest paid officer and in 1969 had been given 100,000 shares of stock at a dollar a share. He had moved his family into the former home of the chairman of the board of Xerox and no doubt expected this to be his final move, the big payoff to a classically successful career. Now he had quit. Why?

In speculating about Karkow's motivations, Jerry revealed more than he probably understood.

"Here's a guy who's a real pro," Jerry explained. "He is making close to seventy-five thousand dollars a year but is not participating in the serious management of the company. He is told what to do by David Stirling and it's driving him nuts. No matter what the outside world thinks, he knows he has become a glorified bookkeeper."

So what does that make you? I asked myself. What have you all become? High-paid flunkies running around that pleasure dome in Bill Blass suits and Cardin ties.

It was strange how my perceptions and Jerry's differed over the same facts. For all the years we had been married, when Jerry had lost jobs and when he had been riding high, we had always shared a common view of what was important in life. Money was important only because it bought freedom and time. It was a means not an end. Obviously Karkow had realized no salary in the world was worth being someone's errand boy. Why couldn't Jerry see *his* growing emasculation as clearly as he saw Karkow's? Why hadn't *he* been the one with the courage to say, to hell with the salary, the stock options, and the way it will look to friends and family if I admit I made a mistake, but I am not being consulted, I am not growing as a lawyer, I am not being challenged, and I quit?

But I fought against feelings of contempt. Most men, I told myself, had to walk that tightrope between taking orders and maintaining their self-respect. Just because a man was restricted in his responsibilities did not mean he was a cipher. That was too adolescent a view of life. But more to the point, wasn't I able to avoid the realities of being an employee precisely because my husband was being paid to face them? Wasn't I being disingenuous about the cost of personal freedom? Hadn't I recently been asked to puff up an advertiser's product and dutifully followed orders rather than risk being fired? So who was the sellout? And would I have been so eager for Jerry to quit if he were working in New York? My motives seemed hopelessly mixed, so I listened and said nothing.

But Karkow's resignation continued to ripple through our lives. We were invited to his home for a good-bye drink. The house, like that of the SantaLucias, was unfurnished. Apparently Mrs. Karkow had never liked the home hastily chosen by her husband, had resisted decorating it, and now could barely conceal her joy at leaving both the house and Rochester. I was tortured by envy. I wanted to embrace her and say, "My god, I know how you feel; I wish I were you." But I only said, "Good luck," and observed, back in the car, how radiant the Karkows seemed. Jerry looked pained, but kept silent.

Finally, on the eve of his departure, Karkow let down his guard in front of Jerry long enough to deliver a few choice blasts at his ex-employers. In his opinion David Stirling was "financially irresponsible," and Yanowitch "unscrupulous."

"Do you think he's right?" I asked, suddenly alarmed and amazed Jerry was reporting this conversation to me.

"I don't know. I honestly don't," Jerry confessed. It was clear he *had* to talk, that in his own way he was trying to grope toward the truth.

Karkow had made no specific allegations. It was an open secret, according to Jerry, that Karkow and Yanowitch had disliked each other from the start, perhaps because they were each vying for David's attention. But Karkow's view of David was so at odds with that held by the rest of the world, so extreme, perhaps it could be explained by the two men's different functions. Treasurers, Jerry pointed out, were trained to be fiscally conservative. David was intuitive; he didn't want to hear why something couldn't be done or hadn't been done before. David Stirling was like an inventor —part visionary, part businessman. Either you believed in his dream or you didn't. Maybe Karkow had simply ceased to believe.

As far as I could tell, Jerry had suffered no serious loss of faith. Whatever private anxieties he may have harbored about Homex's shrinking sales were banished by the confirmation of a second stock offering. It was great news for the company. Another infusion of cash. But it was even better news for Jerry. It meant another prospectus to write. A specific and important work goal. Being back in the center of Homex business. Now that months of do-nothing days were behind him, he confessed what I had long suspected, that he had been bored and underused. He could hardly wait to plunge back into meaningful activity.

Just as the year before, Jerry was now bubbling with good tidings. Mainly about the impressive details of the second offering. This was a big-league operation. Merrill Lynch, Pierce, Fenner & Smith—the largest investment-banking house in the country—was underwriting the sale of 1,025,000 shares of common stock. Peat, Marwick, Mitchell & Co., one of the "big-eight" accounting firms, was preparing the financials. And the capital to be raised was in the vicinity of $20 million as compared to the $6 million of the previous year. The change of underwriters and accountants was described to Jerry as another step up in Homex's irresistible rise to the top. Jerry believed it.

I was delighted for my husband, but recognized if Homex needed a $20-million shot in the arm so quickly after its first, perhaps it had a very expensive habit—which was not good news. Jerry conceded one could view the underwriting in that light. But the main point was Merrill Lynch had not. What they saw was a still-glamorous stock, down from its high of $51.75 per share but steadily traded in the twenties, with an excellent price-earnings ratio, enormous growth potential, and a need to finance that growth. It was an old economic conundrum that, as the daughter of an economist, I should have understood. The essence of monetary health is not cash in hand but the belief, on the part of banks, investors, and underwriters, that the patient is alive and healthy.

Jerry was convinced this $20 million would solve Homex's financial problems for several years. They could repay part of their $35-million bank debt and be assured of continued lines of credit. It would allow the company breathing time to pursue new sales markets, and it would permit Homex to tool-up for assembly-line production of the high rise.

Stirling Homex's 1971 annual report reflected the exquisite optimism of that spring. Rereading it years later is almost like coming across an inspired piece of fiction, but its glossy, pull-out, four-color photographs and projected "opportunities for tomorrow" partially explain why Merrill Lynch, my husband, Peat Marwick, the SEC, and thousands of investors were persuaded to share David Stirling's dream.

Investors were informed of the $3.6 million contract with HUD "to manufacture and install a thirteen-story high-rise building containing more than 200 units at Memphis, Tennessee, for the "Operation Breakthrough" program. . . . scheduled to be completed by June 1972." The report announced plans for a new "$5 million twin-line manufacturing facility at Gulfport, Mississippi," as well as the use of "marine, rail, and highway transportation . . . for marketing throughout the South, Southwest, lower Midwest, and Caribbean area."

What is astonishing, in retrospect, is that not one of the above plans ever came true, not the high rise, the Mississippi plant, marine transportation, nor any sales in new areas. Yet there was ample reason to suppose they were *about* to come true.

The prototype high rise had been built and appeared on the cover of *House and Garden*. A southern sales office was in existence. The previous year a two thousand-foot train had pioneered the transportation of modules by rail. Money had been spent on a scheme to float modules on barges to the Virgin Islands. Senator James Eastland had flown to Mississippi for ground-breaking ceremonies for the Gulfport plant. And in general, there were frequent allusions, within the office, to powerful political connections that would ensure the success of Homex's southern strategy.

Like many businessmen in that pre-Watergate era, the Stirlings and Yanowitch were convinced political pull brought instant results. For years the housing and construction fields had been notoriously corrupt, graft-ridden, and subject to every form of scandal. Builders were frequent contributors to political campaigns and I often wondered if Homex was an exception to the rule. They did not hesitate to staff their Washington office with ex-HUD officials. And, if possible, they sought out politically connected lawyers to represent them, but that was, in American business terms, playing it smart. In private, Jerry sometimes speculated that Homex might be using political pressure, especially in the South. And yet, except for a single indiscretion, when Yanowitch, bursting with self-importance, let it be known he had breakfasted with Frederick LaRue, a wealthy Mississippi Republican and a dollar-a-year Nixon adviser (who subsequently pleaded guilty to a charge of conspiracy to obstruct justice in the Watergate case), Jerry had no idea if or how the company was extending favors. A year and a half later it became public knowledge that not only did Homex jets provide free transportation for senators Eastland, Sparkman, Chiles, and Buckley, but also that it was a Homex jet that ferried Mitchell and LaRue to that ill-fated Key Biscayne meeting in March of 1972, during which, it was alleged, the plan to illegally enter Democratic headquarters was finally approved.

Ironically, these "favors" accomplished nothing. But even in 1971, Yanowitch's awe of political clout, his naïve belief that a complex business problem could be "taken care of" by a call to the governor's office, was openly derided by men within Homex who had spent half their lives in politics. Deals and favors might oil local political machines, but federally subsidized housing was a different ball park. There were too many career civil servants in regional HUD offices, too many community pressure groups, too many zoning boards, building inspectors, and local housing authorities who could, and often did, void a Washington directive.

When Jerry mentioned Harold's hush-hush breakfast with LaRue, I immediately remembered Karkow's parting shot. He had called Harold "unscrupulous." I didn't like the smell of things, but it was equally possible that Harold was only name-dropping.

With the immense task of preparing a second prospectus, Jerry had less time to brood about the company's sales problems and Homex's administrative growing pains. There were more trips to New York, endless conferences with accountants, underwriters, and outside attorneys in addition to assembling and putting into legal prose the facts and figures of the first draft.

With Jerry's legitimate excuse of being overworked, my demands were muted. At least when he was home, he seemed more cheerful and talkative. I was also more relaxed about my work. I no longer worried over deadlines or if I had enough material for a column. If anything, after eight months, I was growing slightly bored and restlessly contemplating greater challenges. I reopened the possibility of a full arts page with my publisher and wrote a lengthy proposal outlining my ideas for new columns and methods of inducing new advertisers. My reputation had continued to broaden. I was now being asked to participate in arts symposiums, to lecture at schools, and occasionally moderate a local TV program. Terrified of public speaking, I labored over my first speech, which went well enough for me to feel another personal barrier had been surmounted. As my self-confidence grew, so did my ambitions. When Andrew Wolfe finally decided he could not afford the kind of broad cultural criticism and news I had envisaged, I began to think of applying for a job at one of the downtown Gannett dailies.

But I resisted such a move until I was certain Homex's second stock offering had become effective. There was always the possibility of something going wrong, of Merrill Lynch changing its mind, the SEC raising objections, or the stock market falling apart. I did not have to be told that our future and the future of Homex depended on its ability to raise $20 million.

In April Jerry received Peat Marwick's seven-month interim audit in connection with his work on the prospectus. He was horrified to discover that Homex had included in its statement of earnings a bizarre land sale that was to account for six out of the twenty-one cents of per-share profits. Con-

vinced the SEC would recognize the sale as an artificial attempt to bolster profits, he pleaded with Harold to take the
matter up with David. Harold could not understand Jerry's
objections. The accountants had agreed to the legitimacy of
the figures. Jerry was not an accountant. Why was he sticking
his nose into this accounting problem? Jerry patiently explained that it was the SEC's duty to separate real corporate
strength from apparent strength. Any fool could see this was
extraordinary income. But even worse, its inclusion might
provoke the SEC's suspicions about the company's entire
financial statement. It was a dumb thing to do, and Jerry
demanded to know what, if any, business reason prompted
such reckless behavior. Harold agreed to talk with David.
Five minutes later he told Jerry, "David wants it."

"Is that the end of the discussion?" Jerry asked.

"That's it," said Harold. "That's all you have to know."

That evening Jerry bitterly recounted what had taken
place. He was appalled not only by David's fiscal manipula-
tion, but also by his refusal to discuss the matter face to face,
and by Harold's total acquiescence to David. Jerry could
have accepted being overruled, he maintained, but it was the
way in which he lost this battle that frightened him. For the
first time he wondered out loud if David was not leading the
company toward disaster.

My chief reaction was: Jerry's pride has been hurt. Jerry
had meant to tell me one story—about a specific, irresponsible business decision; but I had heard quite another—about
his insignificance within the company. There was, I believed,
a moral to this drama Jerry had failed to grasp. If your advice
is being systematically ignored, either you admit the degree
of shit you are willing to take for fifty thousand dollars a year
or you quit.

But again I said nothing. Jerry was too distraught to take
any lectures from his wife. Besides, wives were supposed to
be warm and supportive in moments of stress. After my husband had just had his ego destroyed, how could I say: that
does it, this is the final straw, either you leave that place or
I'm leaving you. It seemed the wrong time and the wrong

issue. I was blowing the incident way out of proportion, inventing reasons for us to go back to New York. I was confused, alarmed, and humiliated by my husband's humiliation.

The preliminary prospectus was filed with the SEC on April 21, a year to the day of our departure from New York. Jerry was exhausted, and since there would be little for him to do until the Letter of Comments was received, we made a last-minute decision to take a vacation. It had been five years since we had ventured on an extended trip without the children. Our part-time baby-sitter agreed to move into the house for ten days. In the middle of May we headed West, to New Mexico and Colorado, to escape the continuing Rochester gloom.

In the past vacations had always brought us closer. This one was no exception. Alone as husband and wife, with money to spend and no business or domestic issues to quarrel about, tensions receded. After so many years of marriage we were bound together by similarities of taste, humor, attitude, and pleasure. One evening, as we again found ourselves ordering identical dinners, it occurred to me that it was like taking a voyage with one's Doppelgänger. There was no need to speak of the harmony, so palpable was its presence. As we silently drove across the parched, scrubby land with its mysterious outcrops of rock, tangerine cliffs, and ink-green forests, we moved as if with one eye in a mutual sea of tranquillity.

Jerry hardly mentioned Homex and I, drifting pleasantly in a kind of vacation mindlessness, felt little compulsion to bring it up. He seemed confident the offering would go through, optimistic about the company's future, and intent on forgetting the stresses of the past year. The farther away from Rochester I got, the happier I became. Waking up to sunshine every day released my brain from its tense, critical, winter-brittle bindings. I could understand why, in such places, one's mind could turn to mush. One did not have to strain for pleasure and beauty. It was enough to be, to soften and grow supple like leather in the sun. My appetite for life, so dulled in Rochester, returned with a rush. I leaped out of bed in the morning full of good humor, an agreeable, affectionate woman who had, for too long, been a resentful grouch.

Vacation moods, I understood, could be as deceptive as early romance. In real life one did not wake up to sunshine every day; one's husband was not relentlessly cheerful and optimistic; one's marriage did not float on a tide of good feelings and self-indulgent play. Yet it was obvious when we were happy—talking, loving, touching—that our mutual generosity, which had been missing, reappeared. Perspectives shifted. The stresses of the past year seemed less significant than the gains. The affection greater than the disaffection. If I could understand, without condemning, Jerry's irrational fear of being stranded on a lonely mountain road, and he could be infinitely sympathetic to my terror of heights —which paralyzed me in the midst of a descent into the Indian cliff dwellings at the Mesa Verde—then why was it not possible for this acceptance of each other's frailties to continue? Clearly the good feelings were there, but we had gotten out of the habit of calling upon them. Vacation euphoria might not be transferable, but its memory would remind us of what was important and good in our marriage. Jerry admitted it had been a mistake not to get away sooner. He had been short-tempered and self-absorbed. The winter had depressed him more than he realized. But now we were back on the track. We were friends and lovers again. It would be June when we returned. Homex would get its money. The summer was coming and the second year in our home was bound to be better than the first. We wouldn't make the same mistakes twice.

CHAPTER VIII

During our absence Rochester had changed. Spring had come and gone in a week and we had missed it. The stock market had taken a sickening plunge. The Letter of Comments had failed to arrive, and there was a barely concealed atmosphere of alarm at Homex.

When word was received that the SEC was about to release its review of the prospectus, Jerry was sent to Washington to relay its contents by phone. He died a little as he read the bad news to Harold and David. As Jerry had predicted, the SEC insisted the land sale be removed from earnings. But far more serious was the commission's opinion that, in general, the company was recognizing profits prematurely. At issue was an accounting practice, which had been established from the beginning of Homex, that had been deemed acceptable by two major accounting firms, two underwriters, their lawyers, and the SEC itself during the company's first stock offering.

The problem was at what point did a manufacturer and installer of houses have the right to declare an order a sale? Homex recorded a sale when a module came off the assembly line and was assigned to a specific housing contract. This accounting profit was taken before a single house in a project had been installed, before zoning, sewage, and other site problems had been resolved, before access roads had been built or a building permit issued. The moment land for a development had been purchased or optioned, and a Letter of Intent from a housing authority proved the existence of a financially capable purchaser, 65 percent of the ultimate purchase price was recorded as income. But since the government never gave progress payments, Homex actually received its monies for subsidized housing when projects were ready for occupancy. This explained the discrepancy between bookkeeping profits and cash on hand.

In its prospectus, Homex defined manufactured but undelivered modules as "unbilled receivables." In 1969 they had amounted to a manageable $644,918, but by the time of the second offering, Homex's unbilled receivables had mounted to almost $30 million, a fact that no doubt contributed to the SEC's concern about the real financial picture at Homex. If the SEC now deemed this accounting practice unacceptable, Homex could not declare an annual profit. Without a favorable earnings picture, Merrill Lynch could never market the stock. Without the $20 million, the company might very well go under.

Only a handful of people understood the thin thread by

which Homex was hanging. Not even Jerry knew for sure what the banks would do if the offering failed to materialize. At the very least they would refuse further credit. It seemed inconceivable they would call their loans, which would force the company into bankruptcy and preclude any possibility of getting back their investment. Nevertheless, it was a serious moment and Jerry confided in no one.

It was the worst month of his life. He barely slept. He felt compelled, at work and with friends, to maintain a constant façade of optimism, and even with me he could not bring himself to express his worst fantasies—the horror of Homex's demise, being stranded in Rochester with a fistful of worthless stock, enormous debts, nowhere to go, and no job to go back to.

Although I had never yearned for disaster, it had occurred to me nothing short of disaster would force Jerry back to New York, so I waited, with hopelessly mixed feelings, for the outcome of a crucial face-to-face meeting between the SEC and a phalanx of Homex advocates. To Jerry's relief the SEC, though unhappy with the accounting practice, rescinded its objections. In return, Homex agreed to drop the infamous land sale from earnings, and a host of minor conflicts were worked out.

While these negotiations were taking place the stock market had continued to weaken. Merrill Lynch decided to switch its offering from common to five hundred thousand shares of preferred stock. Again, there was a frantic rush to rewrite the prospectus before the bottom completely fell out of the market and Merrill Lynch suspended the deal.

I saw very little of my husband for the next few weeks, but it was summer and the children were beginning to spend more of the late-afternoon and early evening hours outdoors. So was I. I had begun, in a modest way, to garden. Last year's threatening jungle of foliage had emerged into bushes and plants whose names and life cycles I was beginning to understand. My domestic sense of order was affronted by what I could now see had once been a gracefully planted landscape ravaged by years of neglect. I could no longer sit outdoors in our cheap garden chairs and ignore the weeds and strangled

flower beds around me. So with the impatient energy of a
neophyte, I attacked the most obvious eyesores—old, un-
pruned rose bushes; peonies that the summer before had
bowed under the weight of their blossoms and required stak-
ing; a patch of pachysandra narrowing our back walk. Then,
having invested in a rake, hoe, hand trowel, and various-
sized clippers, and experiencing the first joys of a house per-
fumed with early summer flowers, I found myself irresistibly
drawn to greater labors and rewards. I put in an herb garden
and four tomato plants. The children scattered radish seeds,
and after dinner, when it was cool, I crouched over my small
plot, breathing the earth, inhaling the smell of tomato leaves,
rubbing basil between my fingers, dreaming of pesto and
omelettes *aux fines herbes.*

There were times that June when, stretched out under our
Chinese elms, I recalled that at this hour in New York, I
would have been dragging myself and two dusty children
from the park. Reluctantly I had to admit that should our stay
in Rochester end, I would miss part of it. What had once been
a simple preference for city over country would never be
that simple again.

In early July Jerry phoned from New York to announce the
imminent completion of the prospectus. Since he would
probably be finished at the printers on a Friday, he suggested
I fly down to New York so we could enjoy a weekend in the
city together. I was to check into the Park Lane—New York's
latest deluxe hotel, favored by junketing Homex executives
and their wives—and Jerry would join me and the Wolfs for
dinner.

I wanted to feel elegant and grand but wound up feeling
totally out of place as I swept into the chandeliered lobby of
the Park Lane in a four-year-old cotton dress and sandals.
There was no use pretending I fit the role of rich, out-of-town
tourist. I didn't, and I was certain the desk clerk with his
continental accent and strained smile of welcome knew I
didn't.

Although Homex would be picking up the tab, and I had
heard from Jerry that a number of his colleagues had been

renting suites and charging everything from cocktail parties to Cardin suits to the company, I chose a room rather than a suite and, out of an inner urge to distinguish myself from the other freeloaders, a back room without a Central Park view.

It was a cheerful, modern room, but I was uncomfortable in it. Returning to New York as a tourist was an unnerving experience. I didn't know what to do with myself. I miserably examined and discarded a variety of activities. I did not want to shop like some suburban matron out on a buying spree. I did not want to dutifully tour the museums like some culture-starved provincial. What I wanted was to plug myself back into the ordinary life of the city, and that was no longer possible.

I walked the streets until my legs ached and then, with more time to kill, ducked into an afternoon movie. When I emerged from the movie house I had come to a major decision. The reconnection to New York that I craved would have to come through my work. Jerry had felt little estrangement from the city because he had always returned to it for professional reasons. His New York days were spent much as before, with business appointments, the usual dashes cross-town and corned beef sandwiches on the run. What if I resumed my free-lance career? Wouldn't that bring me back to the city in a role that was both personally comfortable and professionally challenging? Free-lancing from Rochester would be difficult but not impossible. I had friends and connections in the magazine business. I could get an agent. I had a growing portfolio of feature stories to my credit. Andrew Wolfe, after much hedging, had finally rejected my expansionist ideas for the paper. So now that the stock offering was almost a *fait accompli,* and it was clear we would not be moving back to New York, why not try? It was up to me to get off my ass, plan my future and not wait, like some princess, to be rescued.

By dinnertime Jerry was still at the printers on Hudson Street proofreading the final copy of the prospectus. I went down to the hotel bar to meet our friends. Between the bartender's fresh Margaritas, my delight at seeing the Wolfs

again, and my new career decision, I was decidedly cheerful
by the time Jerry arrived. He was equally euphoric. One look
at his face and I knew panic-time was over. We were ready
to celebrate and proceeded to Le Perigord for an expensive
French dinner. It was then Jerry broke the good news of a
second offering. Peter's only comment was, "Oh, you've already run out of chips." It went through me like a knife.
Peter had seen through this whole drama in a second. When
you set aside the fancy language about land sales, earnings
per share, unbilled receivables, and "creative" accounting
practices, the simple, obvious truth of it all was that Homex
was broke. But if it was so obvious to an outsider, why had
so few people within the company understood? Why hadn't
Merrill Lynch suspected the worst not the best? Perhaps I
would never finally grasp the confluence of risk, profit, fashion, and faith that, at some moment, mysteriously moved the
stock market. Or perhaps it was an irrational game in which
you invented the rules and penalties as you went along? Well,
it hardly mattered. The crisis had passed.

On July 29, the stock offering became effective and quickly
rose from $40 to $54 a share. Back in Avon the morale rose
equivalently—except for Jerry's. I assumed it was a normal
letdown. Opening night was over. But it was more than that.
At first Jerry denied he was depressed or worried, but a few
weeks later two events took place that triggered a revealing
confession. The events themselves hardly struck me as earth-
shaking: Yanowitch had hired a new lawyer, and Homex had
leased a third jet. But they appalled Jerry because, while
preparing the response to the SEC's Letter of Comments, he
had made the unpleasant discovery that the company was
wildly overspending. Jerry had discussed the situation with
Homex's young and newly promoted controller, Edwin
Schulz. Schulz agreed, off the record, there had to be some
fundamental change in the way the company was run. It
could not go on forever manufacturing modules and not in-
stalling them. He also assured Jerry that David Stirling was
aware of the problem. Once the offering was accomplished,
David would refocus his attention to ways of conserving cash.

The manufacturing rate would be cut down. Installation of existing modules would get top priority, even though this might have a temporary adverse effect on earnings. The jets had to go. Executives would be asked not to travel first class on commercial airlines. Expense accounts would be cut back. And so on.

But when Jerry returned to a normal schedule in Avon, he saw that instead of cutting back, just the reverse seemed to be taking place. Why were they hiring another lawyer when, in truth, there was hardly enough work for those already there? Why another jet? Why had the assembly line returned to two shifts when uninstalled modules were wreathing the plant like mushrooms around a dead tree? Business was worse, not better. Federal housing funds, which had flowed so freely under President Johnson's administration, were drying up under Nixon's. Homex did not have a single, secure housing contract in the South, and yet David was still determined to go ahead with the Mississippi plant. Manufacturing more modules that nobody wanted to buy seemed insane.

It all sounded horribly familiar—the premature expansion and inevitable collapse. The compulsion to grow, coupled with a strange refusal to face the economic facts of a shrinking market. Jerry had lived through directly and I indirectly the rise and fall of two law firms. Were we now going to witness the rise and fall of a company? Had Jerry just moved to a bigger trap? I had always harbored my suspicions. Now, those same suspicions were finally dawning on my husband.

A subsequent piece of news convinced me—finally and forever—that the company was doomed. It is always easier, in retrospect, to affix a loss of faith to one hour in one day when, in fact, the process was more cumulative. But the night in August Richard Rosen came to dinner and announced the high-rise hydraulic system had been abandoned because it didn't work, my last bit of faith in David Stirling's dream vanished. I could only compare it to a writer who talks about his book, constructs an elaborate outline, receives an advance from a publisher on the basis of that outline, and then, as the deadline approaches, admits the finished product doesn't exist. I had known several such writers. Crazy artists, we had said. It could only happen in publishing. But George Romney and HUD and the entire "Operation Breakthrough" program had been as conned as any otiose publisher. There might be a fine distinction drawn, in a court of law, between intentional fraud and misplaced optimism, but what responsible company would purport a technological breakthrough, build a four-story prototype, and only when the last ounce of publicity had been squeezed from the creation, quietly withdraw its claims? Either David Stirling was a fool or a lying incompetent, or this was the most elaborate flimflam I had ever seen.

Didn't Richard and Jerry agree? Jerry admitted he was severely shaken. But Richard was bubbling with enthusiasm over Homex's *new* high-rise plan. It was even better than the first, he assured us. A brilliant fall-back position. True, they would erect the high rise through the old-fashioned crane system, but they would prefabricate something called a "wet core." This modular core would contain the expensive parts of the tower—elevators, stairs, bathrooms, kitchens—and go up first. The rest of the structure would be conventionally built. It would still be cheaper than old methods of construction and represent a technological step forward. Homex had asked HUD for a sixty- to ninety-day extension and, with its engineers frantically redesigning plans, would no doubt retain its "Operation Breakthrough" contract.

"Do you really believe that?" I asked.

"Yes, yes, I really do. It's a fantastic idea," Dick insisted, and then spent the rest of the evening trying to explain to Jerry how you prefabricated a "wet core."

I curled up in a corner of the living room and barely listened. As Dick chattered away I found myself wondering how many more stillborn dreams it would take before these two men, both of whom, as it happened, had uprooted their unwilling wives from New York, admitted the enormity of their mistake. Were Richard and my husband clutching at straws out of fear of looking foolish? Of having made tragic career choices? Or was there a profound inability, in even the most intelligent men, to conceive of a company—like a government—collapsing around *them.* Was it impossible for men to admit that they misjudged the nature of the crisis, as well as the nature of the personalities who created it?

Whatever the reasons for their continuing blind faith, I was infuriated by Jerry's loyalty to Homex. This time, when Richard left, I said so.

"If David isn't irresponsible then he's something worse. Don't you see, he would do anything to keep the stock rising. What more proof do you need than this latest fiasco? They'll never build that high rise, and if they do they'll lose money. You've got to leave that place, get out, start looking for another job. Homex is finished. It's a phony. You're clinging to a corpse!"

"Leave to what?" Jerry exploded. "Fifty-thousand-dollar-a-year salaries don't grow on trees. Are you really prepared to give up the way we live, to go back to those six rooms in New York? Who do you think you're kidding? You've gotten used to your nice private office, to this space, to your tomato plants and the tennis club ten minutes away."

"I don't deny it. I won't pretend the adjustment will be easy, but we were happy enough before. Why can't we be happy in New York again?"

"I was making a lot of money when we left. I couldn't walk into a law firm and expect to make that salary again. Especially with the stock market the way it is. They're firing securities lawyers not hiring them, in case you haven't heard."

"But Jerry, you always said if things didn't work out we could go back. That's why we didn't give up the apartment. Are you now saying it's impossible?"

"No, all I'm saying is this isn't the right moment. In fact it's probably the worst moment. If I wait a year I can pick up the first of my options and pay off our debts. Then, if the situation still hasn't changed at Homex, we can figure out what to do next. It would be sheer idiocy to leave now. There's no reason to. So the jacking system doesn't work. So what? They'll think of something else. They always have. I trust Richard's judgment. He's an architect. He understands these technical problems. He's not despondent. He doesn't see the future as bleak. Why do you? Because you want to. Because nothing would give you more pleasure than to see this whole company fall down like a pack of cards."

"You know who you sound like?" I countered, trembling with anger. "Just like Harold and David telling you to keep out of accounting problems because you're no accountant. Well, listen baby, you were right and they were wrong. So don't talk to me about not being an expert. All those god-damn experts are self-serving, self-interested technocrats. And if you're going to start impugning motives, how about yours? The truth is, even if the company turns into a raging success, you hate working for Harold and 90 percent of the time you're bored out of your mind. The truth is there isn't enough for you to do. The truth is we moved for the wrong reasons—not because of the family—but because of *your* fantasies of money and power. Well, you have no power, we're not one bit happier, and we owe more money than we ever owed in our lives. Admit it. Admit you made a mistake. Mistakes happen. It's not the end of the world. Just face up to the realities and clear out."

"You don't know what you're talking about," Jerry retorted. "The subject is closed."

"That's what you think," I shouted, pursuing him up the stairs.

Jerry wheeled and in a deadly calm voice said, "Enough. I've had enough of your Cassandra-like pronouncements for one night. You're screaming. You're in a rage. You are incapable of discussing this subject rationally. I will not discuss Homex or my job or our future one second longer. I'm tired. It's after midnight. I'm going to bed."

It was no use. Either I was crazy or everyone else was, but there were too many layers of conflict between us for Jerry to trust my judgment or for me to trust his.

As usual our quarrel had solved nothing. It had only made matters worse. The well of good feeling from which we had been drawing since our vacation went dry overnight. In its place rose a destructive flood of fury. Our displaced anger was evident everywhere. A tennis game turned into a grim struggle for supremacy. An afternoon walk into a sullen forced march. A day with the children into an elaborate tactical exercise in evasionary techniques. At night Jerry alternated between moods of silent inertia and restlessness that drove him out of the house, after dinner, to a movie or series of bars. I responded to his nocturnal wanderings with the violence of a volcano that had been deceptively quiescent for too many years. I screamed at breakfast when Jerry walked away from a tableful of dishes. I slammed doors, hurled objects, and sneered derisively at fresh news of the company's problems. I experienced a weird sensation of triumph when the "Operation Breakthrough" negotiations finally collapsed. My words, my accusations, my fatal prophecies were becoming palpable realities, and only when Joshua would occasionally come into a room during one of our quarrels and plaintively ask, "Are you two fighting again?" would my anger dissolve into a deeper sense of guilt and terror.

Although part of me was pushing for an ultimate confrontation, when it finally occurred, it was as though a cork had unexpectedly exploded in my hands. A run-of-the-mill argument over changing Jesse's diaper escalated into a raging battle and ended with such open hatred there seemed no room for reconciliation. In a rage, Jerry reverted to his most reactionary, rigid self.

"You lead a goddamn good life," he bellowed. "I am sick of hearing about your oppression, your repression, your burdens, and my duties. You don't know what hard work is. You don't have to get up and go to an office every goddamn day of your life. You have two children. Take care of them. I will not change their diapers. I will not feed them breakfast, lunch, or dinner. I will go out when I want. I will play tennis when I want. I will do nothing when I want. I will go out after dinner for a drink, if I want. That's the way I am. That's the way I've always been. If you think that's unfair, if you can't live with that, then for God's sake get out. Get out!"

Fall 1971

CHAPTER IX

The next day as Jerry silently exited for work I lay immobile in bed trying to sort things out. The murderous anger of the night before had vanished. In its place had come an emptiness and exhaustion reminiscent of the hours after my Caesarean deliveries when I had been sufficiently drugged not to feel pain but knew if I moved everything would hurt.

Although for months I had accused Jerry of every sexist trick and attitude, of the lowest and highest forms of male self-deception, now that he had actually delivered his ringing Victorian ultimatum, I couldn't quite believe it. It was as if a melodramatic fantasy had become real and, once real, no longer made sense. Yes, my husband had said, "If you can't take me as I am then get out," but that cardboard figure uttering that ritual incantation was a caricature of the man I knew. A husband playing the role of husband. A bad guy out of a B-movie. What had been genuine was his pain, bewilderment, and fury. Some unforgivable barrier had been crossed. The marriage had become intolerable and, in a rage, Jerry no longer cared to understand why.

But I cared. Despite my anger and misery it was suddenly apparent I still cared very much. I had not traveled this far to have our marriage explode in a crescendo that was less a confrontation of our problems than an evasion of them. Yes, we were cannibalizing each other, but for reasons we had not

yet faced. And while I had steadfastly clung to the role of
innocent victim, the truth of my complicity could no longer
be denied.

For years I had never seriously questioned the ground
rules of our marriage. I had unthinkingly gone along with the
notion that it was my husband's duty to support the family
financially (which it was not), and that his role automatically
conferred upon him greater value and decision-making powers (which it does not). Only when I agreed to move—which
was less a decision than a mute surrender to the ineluctable
tides of marriage—did I begin to perceive the ramifications
of the trap. If Jerry's job came first, then my life came second.
Implicit in the uprooting had been my tacit acceptance of
marital values, which I had now evaluated and found destructive. But rather than face that fact squarely, I convinced
myself we were not moving for Jerry's career. We were moving for the family. It was not upward mobility in its crassest
sense. I was not a conventional wife about to be hooked and
jerked up out of the sea by the conventional male rod. No,
we were moving on a mutual, noble journey to reinvent
ourselves, to achieve that harmony between work and
family, between labor and pleasure that had become impossible in New York.

But once in Rochester the theory of the noble journey
evaporated. Our move had not been predicated on a mutuality of interest. Our adjustment had not been a mutual effort.
Jerry had not reinvented himself and our family life had
certainly not flourished. I was a camp-follower, no different
from generations of female satellites. Overwhelmed with resentment bred of humiliation, I furiously set about to escape
the shadow of secondary citizenship that had fallen upon me.

But my initial perception of the uprooting as a crime
against me had obscured the whole truth, which was Jerry's
unwitting crime against himself. His refusal to admit the
move had been wrong for both of us, that we were both its
victims, cloaked the essence of our problem: we were in the
classic double-bind of an inequitable marriage. As superwife
I had been futilely trying to establish my worth and regain
my self-esteem in a relationship where money defined

power, while Jerry, having exploited his prerogative as wage earner, found himself locked into the responsibilities he had assumed. He was a prisoner not only of his career mistake but also of those values that had prompted his mistake. In a society where manhood is primarily equated with professional success and sexual virility, failure in either of these areas is failure as a man. Thus, having staked his manhood, his financial future, and his marital dominance on one roll of the dice, he could not admit to himself, his friends, and, above all, his wife that the gamble had not paid off. Jerry had lost on his own terms. He was miserable at Homex, frightened by mounting evidence of corporate incompetence but convinced I would consider him a loser—the world would consider him an improvident fool—if he admitted to an error of judgment.

Like most women, not raised to equate my identity with career conquest, it was difficult to understand the devastating effect of defeat. Jerry could not cope with his feelings of worthlessness. Rather than share his fears, which would mean rethinking his life and staring into an uncertain future, he denied them. The enemy was not himself and his twisted male values, he insisted, but my increasing demands for domestic equality. I had changed, not he. And that was not altogether false.

Ironically and against all odds, the move had liberated me. I *had* reinvented myself. At the very moment Jerry was losing his way, I was rediscovering the direction of my life. Just when my confidence was rising, his was diminishing. Just when my writing was bringing me the external rewards and inner contentment that is the essence of joyful work, Jerry's job had turned into joyless labor. Which meant that just when I was demanding more freedom from the house and children, more domestic sharing and rearranging of roles, Jerry had never felt more enslaved. I had not created his bonds, but that did not prevent him from experiencing them as the unfair bonds of marriage. I had not forced him into a job that was daily torture, but now he was saying, "I will not give more of myself than a paycheck."

The fact that Jerry's money permitted me the job freedom

he had lost only made matters worse. He resented neither
my work nor success, but those values which permitted a
wife, in a leisurely way, to find her vocation at the age of
thirty-three. The rules of male supremacy, with its terrible
pressure upon men to become wage earners, to take no false
steps, had denied him that luxury.

The final irony was that a marriage predicated only a year
before on my sacrifice, was now predicated on his. The bankruptcy of our conventional marriage was complete. But how
to begin again on terms that did not equate a paycheck with
power, that did not give unequal value to our different occu-
pations, that did not make either of us the unwilling slave of
the other?

For months I believed I could draw on the affection and
respect that still existed to restructure our life. I believed we
were too intelligent and committed to our marriage to permit its death. But the miracle of resurrection had not taken
place. Perhaps it had become easier to feel bitter and superior, to play the role of martyr than face my complicity and
guilt. Not only had I missed my opportunity in New York to
assert my rights in this marriage, but also by now I had
become the very person I had accused my husband of
becoming: cold, withdrawn, depressed, emotionally dishon-
est, and uncompromisingly rigid in my views of what I did
and did not owe him as a wife.

I had been acting out of vengeance and wholly distrusted
my motivations. Although I could see the problems, I could
not solve them. Furthermore, did I really want to solve
them? Did I want to destroy my husband or save him? Was
it possible to do one without the other? And even if we
extricated ourselves from Homex, from Rochester, from this
life that had been false and misguided from the beginning,
could I ever care about this man again?

For over a year I had confided in no one. The burden of
that silence had in itself driven me half crazy. But because
our marital difficulties were so intimately related to Homex's,
I had kept my mouth shut. In that sense alone I had been the
model of a good corporate wife. But now, before four lives

were permanently shattered, before the final crunch of bones and flesh, I had to open up.

It was with the greatest reluctance and sense of defeat that I again contemplated turning to a psychiatrist. Why was it always the woman, the wife, who admitted to feelings of despair when both man and wife were in distress? Was this just another example of female dependency? Was it true, as feminists claimed, more women wound up in psychiatric wards because they had been programed to be passive, because they had been denied the emotional mechanisms to deal with the world as assertive grownups? Jerry had said in effect, "Either you change or the marriage is over," and gone off to a day's work. Instead of leaping at the opportunity to clear out, I was lying in bed like a wounded animal. For all my fantasies of independence, superwoman had the courage of a child. Was Jerry counting on that lack of courage to keep me in the marriage on his terms? I didn't know. But since I was living with a man whose very inability to confess anxiety and weakness struck me as self-destructive, might it be an expression of equal cowardice not to seek help? I was beyond being brainwashed by a Freudian who attributed all female anger to penis envy. No one could coerce me into adjusting to a rotten marriage. If after a few months it became clear there was nothing left to salvage, at least I would not berate myself for not having made one last try.

Still, as I reached for the phone, I was acutely aware of the problem of privacy. Rochester is a small town. Half of our friends, as it happened, were psychiatrists. From what I had surmised they were treating or had treated the other half. I used to joke and say, "If I ever crack up, there'll be a stampede of Freudians, Jungians, Reichians, and Behaviorists rushing to save me Their True Way." But now it was no longer a joke. Despite my fondness and respect for these men, and the education I had received listening to them argue the merits and drawbacks of various psychoanalytic techniques, I did not want to meet my analyst, or my analyst's analyst at a dinner party, a situation that had occurred too frequently to others in even the short time I had lived in

Rochester. It was imperative to find someone as far removed from our social circle as possible, someone responsive to my generation's conflicts, preferably eclectic, and a woman.

In New York these conditions could have been easily met. In Rochester women therapists were as rare as honest mechanics and equally in demand. My internist, to whom I turned for advice, was sympathetic but after innumerable phone calls apologetically came up with a list of three men's names. Since two of them sounded vaguely familiar, I chose the third and hoped for the best.

For several weeks Jerry and I continued our lives like actors in a mimed play. On the surface everything was as it had always been, except that I had to force myself to utter the simplest phrases, like, "I'm going to the supermarket," or even, "Good morning." It was like being an adolescent again, living in the same house with an adult one distrusted, wrapping oneself in an impenetrable shield of privacy, begrudging civility lest it be taken for acquiescence or communality of interest. When I finally informed Jerry of my impending visit to a psychiatrist he appeared indifferent, as though it had nothing to do with him. "If that's what you think you need," he said, "be my guest. I even think the company's major medical plan covers psychiatrists. I'll check it out."

"How lucky for you," I murmured, infuriated. I had no intention of making this round of therapy a one-woman show. But I said nothing to Jerry of my intentions. He would show up when requested. What he would never do is admit he welcomed that request.

The psychiatrist's office was located in a mental-health clinic in a modest section of town. In the reception room two-year-old issues of *U.S. News & World Report* were being listlessly thumbed by an assortment of life's losers: teen-agers on methadone, strained-looking mothers whose disturbed children emitted animal noises, old people whose sons and daughters were desperately seeking their admission to various state hospitals.

It was a scene that in no way resembled the suburban, middle-class practices I had come to know. It was depressing and seedy. Like a sane person who finds herself taken to Bellevue, my first impulse was to explain to a passing nurse that a terrible mistake had been made; there was nothing wrong with me and I wanted to be let out. But I sat, eyes on the floor, and grimly waited for my name to be called out, relieved, finally, to be ushered into a narrow, institutional box of an office that looked as if it had been furnished by Allstate. There was no couch, no rug, no window, no fancy furniture. Just three metal chairs, a two-shelf bookcase, and a gray metal desk upon which reposed the prerequisite box of tissues, a phone, and an ashtray. An eskimo soapstone sculpture sat on top of the bookcase and an enormous batik wall hanging of a fiery orange red egg being attacked by spermatozoa stared at me from the opposite wall.

The doctor was probably in his mid-thirties, but had the disheveled, slightly harassed look of a graduate assistant who is holding down two jobs to make ends meet. His wiry gray brown hair rose off a large fleshy face, and his scraggly beard, as unkempt as his hair, gave him a cheering air of informality, which I had not expected. As a staff physician with a quota of private patients, his phone rang frequently and always at the wrong moment. Though to be left hanging in mid-confession felt somewhat like coitus interruptus, I invariably assumed that while others were slitting their wrists, were seriously ill and desperate for help, I was taking up his time with variations on the housewife's lament.

Ten years before, I had entered therapy as a shattered child, with little notion of what to expect and no concept of personal choice. It would never have occurred to me then to "shop around" for a man whose techniques and personality suited my own or to question whether I was receiving the best care. In my circle of friends no one discussed analysts, except disparagingly. It had not yet become fashionable to refer to shrinks or encounter groups. Like divorce it was a shameful admission of failure; like sex it was a subject of mystery and ignorance.

This time I approached my first encounter like a job interview. This is where I am, this is the kind of therapy I want, these are my credentials, what have you got to offer? The doctor understood I would have preferred a woman. Both of us would have to see if we got along. While I was not looking for faddish shortcuts, I envisaged this round of therapy more as family counseling than intense, open-ended personal analysis. It had to include Jerry since, despite my confusion, I was convinced we were equally sick or healthy, depending upon one's point of view.

I viewed the doctor with little awe. I saw him as a trained technician, an expert in seeing patterns and connections, rather than a shaman. He was, I believe, a good doctor, and although we occasionally argued over male and female roles, I never brooded over the fact that I was not in the equally capable hands of a woman. There were times I regretted he was not a female, just as there were times I regretted he was not a New Yorker. So while the therapy was successful enough for me to dispense with it the following fall, I never got over the feeling that the doctor's ignorance about, for example, the mechanics of free-lance writing, reflected the circumscribed community in which he practiced. I sensed, too, that despite my accuracy about Homex, like a great many other people who should have known better, he remained skeptical of my negative intuitions until the end.

It may be, of course, that my disappointment in not finding a Great Man only reflects the exaggerated expectations of any patient toward a psychiatrist. Perhaps I was looking for Big Daddy or perhaps it is a peculiar form of female vanity —like marrying a famous man—that seeks a hero. But at the time I was less aware of my need for heroes than of my being at the entrance of a long tunnel unable to find my way out. If I had any lingering doubts about the doctor's ability to remain impartial because of his sex, they were immediately dispelled the first time he saw me and Jerry together.

It is always an odd moment, introducing one's husband to one's psychiatrist, placing the "real" man next to what had been, until then, one's private and subjective portrait. As a wife I wanted the doctor to like Jerry, to see his qualities, to approve of him, of my choice and thus, of course, to approve of me. But as the aggrieved patient, I did not want the doctor to like Jerry too much. So I was both pleased and distressed when, at our first mutual session, Jerry turned on the charm. Not in months had he been so witty, so gay, so humorously self-effacing, so free of the saturnine temperament I had come to think of as his quintessence. Within minutes the doctor was chuckling at Jerry's one-liners, then roaring with laughter at his business jokes, struggling to preserve his professionally aloof manner but, like a child, erupting into high-pitched giggles again and again.

"Dammit," I thought, "the doctor's really falling for him. I've had it." I also noted, with some envy, the doctor had never laughed with *me,* but while I was contemplating my jealousy, the doctor finally said, "You're a very funny man, but of course you realize what you've been doing," and I knew joke time was over.

Jerry looked quite startled. "Doing?" he asked.

"Yes. Just now. Here." The doctor was still wiping tears of laughter from his eyes.

"I don't get what you're driving at." Jerry glanced at me for help, saw he wasn't going to get it, and froze.

"Yes you do," said the doctor, amicably.

Jerry folded his arms across his chest and tilted his chair on its back legs as though he were waiting for a fellow lawyer to illuminate a particularly fine legal point. There was a long silence as we all stared beyond each other's shoulders. I was determined to say absolutely nothing.

"I'm referring to the way you *use* your sense of humor," the doctor volunteered at last. "It's a very effective shield, but a shield nonetheless."

"So I've been told by my wife." Jerry rocked on the precarious tips of the chair's straight legs, a wary look on his face.

"But you don't agree?" the doctor persisted.

"I don't think anyone can accuse me of being a barrel of monkeys lately. I don't think I've been laughing problems off."

"Yes, but in general . . ."

"In general," said Jerry, "I think it's a sign of my sanity."

Observing the doctor was like watching, after years of amateur productions, the performance of a pro. As yet the play held no surprises. It was too early for revelations of character, but the manner in which lines were delivered caught my attention. I had forgotten what it was like to probe without wounding and to pursue a point without being distracted by debater's tricks. I had never been very good at keeping cool. I tended to wildly fling out my accusations like an ignorant gardener with seeds, hoping one or another would take root. But here was the doctor amicably zeroing in on a single point, and if Jerry was not agreeing, he was at least listening. Of course Jerry trusted the doctor's objectivity, but what I discovered or rediscovered over the next weeks and months was that there were ways of expressing emotion that engendered trust. To say, "I sense something is troubling you," is very different from saying, "For chrissake, what's wrong now." To say, "I must tell you your abruptness over the phone upset me," is far better than seething silently and greeting one's husband, who has probably forgotten the incident, like ice. As a person for whom language, for whom the naming of emotions and gradations of feeling had always represented a sacred task, the challenge of communicating rather than hording my perceptions appealed to my temperament.

All of this was very simple to comprehend but, like many aspects of living that appear simple, it was not at all natural. It was rather like observing a lithe body skip, bend, and drop into a perfectly balanced *plié*, then, at home, trying to imitate the movement. Besides, I thought to myself, this was mere technique. Yes, we might learn to communicate more openly, but we were only dealing with minor irritations and misunderstandings. When were we going to get to what lay beneath them?

What I foresaw, I suppose, was a formal conference, a deliberate setting aside of time to discuss "the move," its reasons, its implications, what we both expected, what we got and why. I had first consulted the psychiatrist in early

September. It was now late October and Jerry and I still seemed to be at a standstill. Each of us was getting better at using words to convey the superficial irritations of marriage. But arguments about diapers and dishes were getting us nowhere. These were symptoms. Jerry would still not discuss the realities of Homex. He refused to admit the move was a mistake, or undertaken on the basis of assumptions. He shied away from any but the most superficial expressions of tenderness.

Ironically, he enjoyed our sessions together with the psychiatrist. They were islands of time away from the children, daylight hours as opposed to after-work, after-bedtime-story hours, when for a few moments, after we emerged from the clinic together we could enjoy an aimless adult ride or uninterrupted chat. Jerry would put his arm around me and say, "I like being with you alone. You know I still love you and admire you," and although I responded to his warmth I knew it was not enough. Affection, though a necessary beginning, was not the point. Not by a long shot. The deeper conflicts lay buried like land mines. I felt I could step on them whenever I wished. I knew exactly where they lay. Jerry did not. But I was terrified of the explosion. It would mangle us beyond repair. What was needed were small, controlled convulsions, little wordless shocks administered by someone else, by a doctor who knew what he was doing.

I was waiting, then, in a state of tension and self-imposed silence for the doctor to gingerly open Pandora's box. Instead, one day, he asked if we had ever heard of something called a "trust walk." Each partner, he explained, takes a turn blindfolding the other and leads him or her through unfamiliar terrain. My God, I remember thinking, one of those crazy California games. How idiotic! And then I'll have to find a baby-sitter, and the children will wonder where we are going on a Saturday morning without them, and we'll have to make up some ridiculous story. But feeling rather peculiar, I made the necessary arrangements. At the last minute we almost forgot the blindfold. I rushed back upstairs and found the red bandanna we had bought in Durango the year before. We'd never had any sensible use for it anyway. I stuffed it into my coat pocket and went back out to the car, to the luxurious company Chrysler, where Jerry sat waiting.

"Well, where to?" he asked, obviously ill at ease. Why me? I thought. Why do *I* always have to figure everything out? He's the goddamn executive.

"Highland Park is nearby," I volunteered.

"How do I get there?"

It was too much, this inability of Jerry's to cope with the little details of life. "You've been there a dozen times!" I exploded.

"Look," said Jerry, evenly, "if you want to go through with this thing, just give me the directions. If not, I'll turn around and go back."

We found the park, which was five minutes away. It was a chilly morning, few people were around, but instinctively we headed away from the parking area, down a narrow, wooded trail that opened onto a sloping hill.

"Let's start here," I finally suggested, when it was clear Jerry could not bring himself to begin. "You blindfold me."

Jerry gingerly wrapped the bandanna around my eyes. Then he led me up and down the hill for about five minutes until there seemed no further point in going on. I had felt nothing, except a certain amusement. How funny we must both look! Now it was my turn to blindfold Jerry. He was too tall for my reach and I asked him to bend down. When he straightened up, he held on to my hand with a steely grip, as though he were afraid of falling.

First I went up the hill. The sounds of children's voices became louder. Jerry stiffened. "I don't want to go where people can see us."

"Okay, okay," I murmured, half-giggling, half-contemptuous. I turned him around, suddenly feeling like the mother in a game of Pin the Tail on the Donkey. A tall, black man was sitting on the other side of a ravine, watching our strange behavior. I decided not to tell Jerry we were being observed. We moved downhill now. I was having a good time, pulling aside branches, zigzagging across the terrain. I liked being the leader. Jerry moved like a man who had just recovered from a stroke. He took small, tentative steps and gripped my hand even harder. Suddenly, he refused to budge. He seemed afraid I was about to throw him into a gorge.

"What's wrong?" I asked.

"Where are you taking me? It's too steep."

"See for yourself." I removed the bandanna. We were on a small incline, in the middle of a trail that must have been formed by thousands of children running up and down the hill. There was no abyss except in my husband's mind. He had been terrified—of what? Of me, certainly, but also of the powerlessness of his condition. For a brief span of time the roles had been reversed, physically and in far more subtle ways.

Jerry looked dazed, genuinely bewildered by what had just taken place.

"You really thought I was going to throw you overboard?"

"Yes, I guess so," he admitted.

I felt strong and calm. The anger had gone out of me. I felt we were strangely suspended in time and that at last the male and female masks had been set aside. I had not foreseen that this "trust walk," from which I expected nothing and had agreed to out of a sense of obligation, would prove so shattering, would break through to that secret room within Jerry I had been yearning to enter.

After the walk, during which there had been little trust but from which it would miraculously flow, we sat on a park bench at the top of a small hill that gave an uninterrupted view of the city. The sky, as usual, hung like a pale gray shroud over a flat jumble of homes and factories. It had been two years since I had first set foot in Rochester, and I was still as unreconciled to my presence as when we first arrived.

We sat in total silence for a long time. Rochester had never looked uglier. In summer its lush, immense trees would have screened our eyes from the grimness of such a view. In fall the oaks and maples blazing with color might have given us a false sense of rural splendor. But the trees were now bare and I sensed Jerry shared my estrangement.

"Do you think our children will think of themselves as Rochesterians?" Jerry asked wistfully.

"They're bound to," I sighed. "They already have Rochester accents. It's horrible, that nasally *a*. It sounds like they've got rocks up their nose."

Jerry had not shaved. His skin was the color of parchment. His shoulders were hunched up and for a moment I thought, as he stared down at the ground, he was going to be ill. But perhaps it was the effort of finally putting words to locked-up feelings that gave him such a look of anguish.

"It's unreal. This whole year has been unreal," he murmured at last. "What the hell happened? I did everything a man is supposed to do. I followed the rules. I consulted everyone I knew. All I wanted was to get away from the insanity of New York, to make a better life, and here I am in a situation that's even crazier than before."

"Maybe they weren't the right rules, Jerry. And maybe we've been horribly unlucky."

"I guess I've always believed in luck. I've gotten my best jobs through luck, coincidence, being in the right place at the right time. Maybe something will happen to bail me out again."

"Not this time," I said, as gently as I knew how. "You can't wait around forever. You know that."

Jerry nodded grimly. Then he began to talk. Not about us, not about the marriage, but about the dream that had brought us to this chilly, gray city, the dream of wealth and success, the great lure of flash and money and emotional fulfillment that was turning into a terrifying nightmare. He talked about the one thing he had refused to discuss frankly, the baffling situation at Stirling Homex.

"I suppose I've been praying the company would straighten out and get over its growing pains. I mean most companies, close up, have pimples and warts and worry lines and dark circles under their eyes they try to cover up. But it's like a goddamn madhouse out there. A fucking zoo. You have no idea what it's like. One day the treasurer tells me he's worried about meeting the payroll and the next day I find out David's bought himself another jet!"

"My god, I didn't know things were that bad. But the company just got $20 million. What's happened to it?"

"For starters, we still owe the banks $35 million. Then we've got an incredibly high overhead, and David keeps turning out those modules and assigning them to so-called projects that never get built. And he's still dead serious about that Mississippi plant which, as far as I can see, will only turn out more houses nobody will buy."

"What do you mean? I thought there were all those hurricane victims in Mississippi desperate for housing?"

"Well, the *people* may be desperate, but the point is our houses are too expensive for the southern market. We have never yet won a competitive bid in the South because of our price, and there is no way a politician is going to pick a high bidder who pays northern union wages. It would be political suicide. So our houses can be assembled faster. So what? Nobody really cares if a bunch of poor people live in trailers or shacks for a few more years. Besides, our wood materials are wrong for the southern climate. The whole deal is hopeless."

"But if you know that, doesn't David know too?"

"He gets the information. Harold gets the information. But then they pretend they haven't heard or it doesn't matter. Maybe they think their connections with Eastland and La-Rue will pay off. It's weird."

"But what about those modules that were hauled by train to Corinth, Mississippi, and got so much publicity?"

"That was a one-shot emergency deal. But you notice we haven't built any more houses in that town. And we were supposed to. Somehow it hasn't happened. Whenever I suggest to Harold that, perhaps, building a plant in the South isn't feasible, he says, 'Don't worry. We're working on it. It's being taken care of. You just draw up the papers and be prepared to move fast' or some horseshit like that."

"I don't know how you can stand it."

"I don't think I can very much longer. It's eating up my insides."

"Then get out! Start looking for another job. I'm not asking you to quit tomorrow, but why don't you face the fact that even if Homex survives, you are miserable there. You don't respect Harold and David anymore. You've got nothing important to do. It's a dead end."

Jerry put his arm around my shoulder. "Yes, I'll have to do something, but the question is what." I snuggled into the curve of his body. "If I put out feelers in Rochester I'll be fired the next day. I know. I've seen it happen to other guys. This is a very small town and David is wired into it. But there're no jobs in New York. The new-issue market is dead. But even if it weren't, I'm not sure I'd want to get involved in that hustle again. And what if I go to a headhunter and he asks me if I'm willing to relocate to Tucson. Am I? Are you? Are we in any condition to go through *another* move?"

"I can't answer that in the abstract," I replied. "But nothing could be worse for us than where you are now."

"There's one other possibility . . ."

"Let's walk around a bit," I suggested. "I'm freezing."

". . . forcing the Stirlings out."

For a moment I was too startled to speak. Of all Jerry's options, that seemed the craziest. "How on earth could you pull off a stunt like that?"

"To begin with, it wouldn't be just me. I'm convinced the new treasurer, Paul Kuvecke, is not one of David's yes men. He's been talking to me privately. We get along. And I get the impression he doesn't trust the information he's been getting from David. Paul's a key man. It's his job to report our financial condition to the banks, and if he told them the Stirlings were running the company into the ground, the banks might be able to force the Stirlings to resign."

"Sounds like something out of *Executive Suite.*"

"The maddening thing is," Jerry went on, as if talking to himself out loud, "I still believe we have a good product, we have a lot of good will, we have a lot of good people who are willing to work very hard for the company. The business could be saved if it weren't being run with one eye on Wall Street. If it only had intelligent, sane management."

We were back at the car. Jerry leaned against the front fender, his arms around my waist, staring above my head.

"But you'd have to *prove* David and Harold are incompetent or consciously misleading everyone," I said. "I've learned *something* being a lawyer's wife. You'd need evidence. Do you have any or how would you get it?"

"I'm not sure," Jerry replied, obviously turning over possibilities in his mind. "I'll have to think about it."

As much as I hated to end the conversation, I knew we had to get back. I had told the baby-sitter we'd only be gone for an hour and it was already lunchtime. "Listen, we can continue this later, but I'd rather lose a husband than a good baby-sitter."

Jerry laughed, then looked down at me and said, "It's been quite a morning, hasn't it? I guess that doctor knows his stuff."

"I guess so."

"I've been pretty impossible these last few months, haven't I? I'm sorry. I really am."

"I know you are. I know it's been hell."

"God I feel tired," said Jerry. "Drained."

"Do you? Well, I feel great. This is the first intelligent conversation we've had since we came to this godforsaken place."

"I'll never figure you out. Here I've just admitted I'm at the end of my rope, my life is a tragedy, and you couldn't be happier."

Jerry was smiling and so was I.

CHAPTER X

The therapy was taking effect far quicker than I had thought possible. We had by no means solved all our problems, but at least each quarrel, each confrontation brought us closer to an understanding of what we both wanted from each other, what we could and could not live with, and what the price was for failing to express our needs honestly. Above all, Jerry was now speaking openly about the situation at Homex. In that area of our lives, we were viewing the future from the same side of the fence.

However, just when the possibility again arose of our having to move, my career again took another leap forward. So that underlying discussions of the future was our awareness that relocating *now* might be the very worst thing for me.

In the fall I had heard the job of cultural reporter for the Gannett's morning paper would soon become vacant. I did not want a full-time job, especially one that involved, as this one did, late-night deadlines. I had no confidence I could dash off a posttheater or postdance review in an hour, or that I would even enjoy trying, but I saw clearly that I had outgrown my present work, and further growth meant taking whatever challenges were available.

I applied for the job and trotted down to the massive, block-long building that housed the Gannett press and its flagship papers, a briefcase bulging with my, by now, impressive collection of clips. But I was prevented from making what probably would have been a career mistake by a perceptive managing editor who realized my talent lay in feature writing. Would I be interested in free-lance work for the *Democrat and Chronicle*'s Sunday magazine supplement, *Upstate?* It was, in fact, a perfect solution to my problem, for with a steady stream of local assignments I could quit my job and use the rest of my time to reassault the national magazines.

I had never thought of such a possibility before because *Upstate* rarely used outside talent. And it was obvious when I first spoke to the woman who edited the magazine that she was not used to dealing with competent free-lancers. Was I, her expression suggested, one of those bored housewives who had taken it into her head she could write? But once she perused my clips, her doubt changed to something like awe. I had written for *The New York Times*. The waves parted. I realized with a pang that I could have successfully approached the Gannett press a year before. I would have roared with laughter at the thought that my credentials provoked respect. In New York they would have occasioned some interest. Here, I was the proverbial big fish in a little pond. I understood its limitations, but it was pleasant to discover, coming from a city where the competition among free-lancers is fierce, that in Rochester I practically had the field to myself.

Until I carried out my first assignment—a profile of a local artist—no long-term commitments would be made. I did not quit my job, but was confident that, within a month or two, I could.

So while part of me couldn't wait for Jerry to leave Homex, part of me was reluctant to surrender the promising situation I had set up for myself. And part of me belatedly recognized that Rochester's dreary weather and lack of distractions were an ideal setting for work. Holed up in my attic office day after day I never felt I was missing out on life, that writing was a deprivation. It was, in fact, my salvation. Could I so cheerfully lead a monastic existence in a city where the sun beckoned and pleasure lurked in the streets? But it was pointless agonizing about an abstract future dilemma. It was difficult living in this no man's land of uncertainty, but in some ways I was happier not knowing where we would be in a year's time. I could bear the coming winter thinking that, perhaps, it would be my last.

Whether due to the effects of therapy or Jerry's simple recognition that we could not repeat our previous blunders, he capitulated on the issue of skiing. We would try it. We would not invest a fortune in equipment, but would join three couples who were returning to a family ski resort in the Canadian Laurentians Christmas week. We could rent skis. There were morning and afternoon classes for all ages and levels. It was a relatively inexpensive package deal, and it would give us something to look forward to, a respite from the increasingly desperate situation at Stirling Homex.

By December a kind of deathly calm had settled over the executive wing. Although dozens of deals were always pending, although an atmosphere of frenzied activity persisted in certain sections of the company, there was less and less for the legal department to do. And yet, as is perhaps always true when a company is in grave danger, no one allowed himself to believe it. The demise of Stirling Homex was as unthinkable as a nuclear war. It was alluded to. An in-bred gallows humor arose, but still, up to the very end, everyone believed their leader, like some all-knowing protective father, would save the situation.

That so much naïveté could be assembled under one roof is, even in retrospect, astonishing. Perhaps it was a result of greed, another facet of the stupidity and blindness engendered by dreams of wealth, plus the fear that one might be wrong and prematurely abandon ship. By this time Jerry was cautiously expressing his fears to my father and a few lawyer friends in New York. They all said, "Things probably look worse than they are. All companies experience ups and downs. Don't act hastily. Don't panic." And so forth. The conventional wisdom was as wrong as it had been two years before, but its effect was to make Jerry hesitate before taking any irrevocable action. Because of the secretive way the company operated, because of the type of people who had been hired to run it, no one, including my husband, knew the worst, and it seemed unlikely the truth would ever come out.

Of the nineteen men listed in the 1971 annual report as "Management," none had any previous experience at the highest levels of business. Seven were lawyers, drawn from private practice and government service; two had never worked for anyone but David Stirling, and the rest were an assortment of middle-echelon salesmen, engineers, accountants, and computer types whose salaries had practically doubled within months of arriving at Homex.

When the company's fortunes were rising, it was easy to overlook the inexperience of the staff. Everyone's amateur status contributed to the intense enthusiasm at Homex; they were young revolutionaries about to set the establishment on its ear. Yes, the place was disorganized, but so, no doubt, were all businesses when you really saw them from the inside. Besides, David Stirling was living proof that a man didn't need a string of college degrees to build a public corporation. Professionalism was a myth perpetuated by academics, but here was foxy David again triumphing over Goliath. If David Stirling was an amateur, then the business world needed more amateurs. So in the beginning when Tommy Santa Lucia and Jerry would get together and shake their heads over some bit of office stupidity, when Jerry would joke and say about the company, "It's like amateur night at the Bijou," no one took it very seriously.

But it soon became apparent to the lawyers that their boss, Harold Yanowitch, was a living embodiment of that maxim, "In the land of the blind, the one-eyed is king." Even in the best of situations, a general counsel navigates through treacherous channels. He must vigilantly defend the best interests of his company without totally identifying himself with those interests. He must uphold the law; be prepared to risk his job by insisting on procedures and disclosures that may not put a company in its most favorable light, which is why corporate officers often have as much fondness for their general counsel as for their dentist. But the minute a general counsel prefers a marriage of love to a marriage of convenience his value as a legal guardian of the public interest is over.

Lawyers in private practice have traditionally reserved their greatest contempt for corporate attorneys, on the assumption it is impossible to serve one master and the law at the same time. While it has yet to be proven that legal venality is related to whether a man is beholden to one client or many, it is true that if a general counsel confuses loyalty to his boss with loyalty to the law, the consequences may not simply be disastrous to two people—a private tragedy—but to vast numbers of innocent people—the investing public.

What had at first seemed Harold's greatest assets—his fierce loyalty to David Stirling, the Messianic quality of his belief in the company and its future—turned out to be his greatest failing. Like many men who have made it their mission in life to carry out orders, to prostrate themselves before genius, to link their wealth and careers to the success of someone else; like all those superstraight, conservative,

law-and-order men in the Nixon White House, Harold failed
to separate ends from means, loyal opposition from disloyalty. So it is not an exaggeration to suggest that Harold the
courtier became, next to David Stirling, a chief cause of Homex's demise. The man without whom, as they say, none of
what happened would have been possible.

In the weeks before we left for our ski vacation at "Gray
Rocks," Jerry's relationship with Harold became icily formal
and I hadn't seen much of Joan since I went back to work.
There was not an overt falling out. The estrangement grew
until it became clear to Harold that Jerry's feelings toward
him had undergone a radical change. Sensing Jerry's diminished esteem, Harold naturally relied more on other members of his staff, especially the most-recently hired lawyers
who were still eager to please and less aware of the dark
undercurrents within the company. Which left Jerry with
even less to do and more time to brood.

Now that Jerry had made the simple discovery that my
respect for him was not dependent on some impossible standard of career success, now that he felt free to confide his daily
anxieties and humiliations as well as his realistic fears about
the future, our marriage, like a repotted plant, developed in
the rich soil of trust. Jerry's job dilemma became our job
dilemma, and as I reached out to support his needs, he
reached out to share mine. He offered to bathe the children
on those nights it was clear I was exhausted from work; he
volunteered to set the dinner table before a party and did not
have to be urged to clean up; he consciously set aside more
time to play with the children, and, perhaps because his job
gave him little pleasure, family relations again became a
positive force in his life.

In our new mood, we could hardly wait for the ski trip. It
was to be our first family vacation, a test of Jerry's renewed
vision of togetherness. It also loomed in our minds as a water-
shed, for Jerry had resolved, in that arbitrary way people
sometimes do, he would make a firm decision about his job
after the Christmas break. So it came as a particularly un-

pleasant shock to discover that, at the last moment, the Yanowitches decided to join their Rochester friends for a week of
skiing at Gray Rocks. They were to fly up with David Stirling,
whose ski lodge was less than an hour from our resort, in the
company plane, a fact that further set Jerry's teeth on edge.
The planes were Jerry's *bête noire*. Nothing enraged him
more than their existence and the way in which the Stirlings
used them for their private convenience, to fly to New York
or Miami for the weekend, to transport their families to the
Bahamas or Canada, or placed them at the disposal of politicians and developers for God knew what favors in return.
Jerry was desperate to get away from Harold, to evade, if
only for a week, the debilitating effects of constant dissem-
bling. But it was too late to change our plans if for no other
reason than to do so would raise questions in everyone's mind
as to the true relationship between Harold and Jerry. Besides, our son Joshua had been counting the days until this
great adventure began, and to disappoint him would have
been unthinkable.

The ski week turned out to be far more grueling than I had
anticipated—more like basic training at Parris Island than
basic pleasure. We were up at seven, out on the slopes by
eight thirty, back for a quick lunch and then, just when I was
ready to collapse, I would have to force my body back into
four layers of clothing for afternoon classes, which lasted till
four. When the thermometer shot to five above zero, it was
greeted as a tropical heat wave. A group picture of our class,
snapped on the coldest day of the week, captured my frozen
smile and Abominable Snowman grace. Ironically, my enthusiasm diminished with each passing day and Jerry's increased. But unlike the competitive stress that had often
developed between us on a tennis court, neither of us suc-
cumbed to what I perceived was another arena for male-
female rivalry. In fact, as on our vacation out West, confiding
our weaknesses strengthened our intimacy. I was, as I should
have known, more afraid of going up the mountain than
coming down. The T-bar held more terrors than a fifty-foot
drop, and when our little group of beginners was advanced

enough to take the chair lift, I simply prayed I would not break down and make a total fool of myself.

This daily self-punishment of body and spirit was mitigated by that vaunted après-ski life I had, for so many years, been hearing about. While Gray Rocks was hardly St. Moritz, my agility on a dance floor definitely outshone my stem-Christies, and whatever miseries I had endured that day could, at night, be transformed into humorous tales of survival.

We managed to see very little of the Yanowitches. Joan was virtually confined to bed with a bad back and Harold, who drove himself down the toughest slopes, rarely stayed up to dance or drink at night.

One evening, however, six couples, including Harold and Joan, journeyed to a nearby French restaurant for what had been promised to be a spectacular meal. The restaurant looked like one of those quaint country inns pictured in travel brochures, but instead of the expected wood-burning fireplace and copper-kettled charm, its interior resembled a vast Floridian sun porch. It was like stepping off of an iceberg into a greenhouse, and the effect on me of a tiled floor, wicker furniture, and a jungle of flowering plants was instantaneous. I became completely manic—laughing, chattering, and quaffing martinis with gay abandon. I was later told the food was indeed very fine. I wouldn't know. As the second course was placed before me I turned crimson, then lime green, quickly excused myself, retched in a series of basement rooms, and passed out. It was the most fortuitous drunk of my life because after the feast Harold invited the group to David Stirling's chalet for a nightcap. Jerry was delighted to have me as an excuse for his nonappearance at an event that was subsequently described as exceedingly awkward.

When the week was over, Jerry and I congratulated ourselves on how well we had maintained our façade. No one had the slightest inkling that Harold and Jerry were barely speaking. There had been no ugly scenes, no flares of temper. But within a few months of the new year, the inevitable confrontation would take place.

Winter–Spring 1971–1972

CHAPTER XI

Two weeks after our return from Gray Rocks, David Stirling, Sr., died. Father Stirling, as he was called around the company, had been well liked and, in this era of the generation gap, admired for the exceptional devotion he had engendered in his two sons. That three generations of a family could live in harmony next door to one another was, I believed, a tribute to their humanity, so I agreed, out of a last shred of propriety toward the Stirlings, to accompany Jerry to the funeral home in Avon where, I presumed, hundreds of other employees and their wives would be paying their last respects. But to my surprise the parking lot was empty, the funeral home almost deserted, and in the gloomy room containing the open casket only David and Bill were present, silently standing side by side as if on a receiving line before a formal party.

Even in normal times the brothers were noticeably different in appearance. Bill was tall and graceless, like a dark, beefy animal already running to fat. At thirty-three, six years younger than David, he looked like an unfashionable country cousin whose lack of style relegated him to an older generation.

As we approached the two men I was again struck by their dissimilarity. Bill was a wreck. His face was red and puffy, his clothes disheveled; he shifted his weight from foot to foot in

an agitated manner and wore dark glasses to hide his emotion. David, on the other hand, radiated an extraordinary air
of tranquillity. He could have glided out of a Paul Stuart
catalog as he accepted, with a small smile, our few words of
sympathy. I was affected by Bill's anguish, but equally relieved not to be faced with the spectacle of David Stirling
going to pieces before me. I mistook it for a sign of inner
strength. A month later, when I discovered the source of
David's serenity, my judgment about the brothers, about
who was weak and who tough, would be reversed.

After we murmured our condolences, the large dim room
again returned to total silence. I was rigid with embarrassment and terrified we might be asked to view the body. The
four of us stood staring blankly at each other until David had
the grace to say, "Thank you for coming," and we felt free
to retreat to the entrance hall of the funeral home where a
handful of minor Homex functionaries were milling about.

I recognized no one, but Jerry nodded in various directions
and then paused to chat with an enormous man who looked
like a bouncer and, in fact, turned out to be one of the company's ubiquitous security staff. We were introduced. He
seemed eager to engage Jerry in conversation.

I stood a few feet away as wives often do when their husbands run into unknown co-workers. Although I was used to
such encounters, where the small talk made little sense and
the office jokes seemed less than funny, this conversation was
more opaque than usual and I found myself straining to
figure it out.

The security man was talking about a recent weekend in
New York City. I expected to hear the usual great-place-to-
visit routine, instead I thought I heard him say he had spent
four days in a hotel room meditating with a bunch of long-
haired hippies. I was puzzled and thought perhaps I had
misunderstood, since he hardly looked like a candidate for
transcendental meditation. Besides, he was chuckling as he
talked, so I assumed he was only kidding around. But then he
added that his boss had flown down on the company plane
and meditated too.

"He couldn't stand being in the same room with all those unwashed creeps," the security man confided. "He was sure they were all high on pot." At this he laughed, then, remembering where he was, abruptly stopped. "Yeah, it was some scene," he mused, "but what can you do? When the big man says, 'Try it,' you try it, right?"

Jerry was smiling in a way that made me assume he understood the conversation, but he didn't pursue the subject, asked a few perfunctory questions about how the Stirlings were taking the strain, and we soon left.

I was bursting with curiosity and expected Jerry to explain this bizarre exchange after we got back into the car. But he said absolutely nothing. I couldn't figure out what was going on. Had they been referring to a secret Homex training program? Had I totally misunderstood the nature of the exchange? Or was Jerry trying to keep something from me because it would put him or the company in a bad light? As we drove through the frozen countryside I became convinced his silence was a deliberate exclusion and I became increasingly furious. Nothing had changed after all. Jerry was still a man from whom speech had to be extracted like a painful tooth. He was still, instinctively, a withdrawn, uncommunicative human being, and the anger of a thousand past silences welled up. This time, I said to myself, I will not allow that poisonous cycle of secrecy, mistrust, and estrangement to begin again. Although it took an enormous and unnatural effort, I spoke.

"What the hell was that man talking about?" I demanded, forgetting all the psychological niceties. "How can you just sit there and not say a word?"

Jerry looked genuinely startled, as though I had interrupted a quite different reverie. His mind was obviously on something else, but he knew what I was referring to.

"You mean that stuff about going down to New York?"

"Of course that's what I mean. What in God's name are you trying to keep from me now?" I was so tense, my body felt like a knotted rope.

"Keep from you? I'm not trying to keep anything from

you. It just seemed so trivial, I didn't think you'd be interested."

"You know, Jerry, it often puzzles me how a sensitive man can frequently be so insensitive to his own behavior. How would you feel if a friend came up to me and said she'd been meditating all weekend, and I said nothing about it. Wouldn't you be faintly curious? Wouldn't you wonder what was going on and why I failed to mention this unusual bit of personal information?"

"Not really."

"Well, that's the difference between you and me. I am interested in people, and in your life, and if you can't talk to me about what's going on in your world, what's left but two strangers sharing the same house but nothing more?"

"Okay, I get the point."

"I wonder if you do, if you realize how your silence isolates yourself from me, and from friends as well. But in any case, why *did* David send a planeload of security men to New York City to meditate?"

"To learn to relax."

"What?"

"You asked, so I'm telling you."

"Do they have ulcers or something?"

"No, it's just that David and Harold have gotten hooked on some mind-control course—whatever that is—and now they want everyone at Homex to take it. I just heard about it a few days ago myself."

"But the security man was talking about hippies and pot. That doesn't sound, if you will forgive the pun, like David and Harold's speed."

"Nothing would surprise me about those two anymore."

"But what's this course about? What do they do?"

"All I know is that it has something to do with alpha waves, if that means anything to you."

"Alpha waves?" I was flabbergasted. "I don't believe it."

Now it was Jerry's turn to sound annoyed. "You don't believe what?"

"That David and Harold would get involved in such a way-out thing."

"Okay, educate me. What the hell *are* alpha waves?"

It was remarkable that my husband had never heard of alpha waves. We both read three papers a day, including *The New York Times*, as well as a variety of weekly and monthly magazines ranging from *The New Republic* to *Esquire*. One of our closest friends in New York had even written on the subject while writing an article on sleep research, but by 1972 it had moved from the world of scientific journals to popular cultism. Like TM and yoga, classes in "instant-meditation" were proliferating like health spas. Even in the local press, advertisements were beginning to appear that promised to "expand your talents, improve your skills, develop your mental abilities, effect positive changes in your personality, and correct disturbing habits through understanding your own mind."

As I explained to Jerry what I had read about electrical patterns of brain activity, about how the lightest level of sleep was defined as an alpha state, about how people "in alpha" had been taught to control the so-called involuntary reflexes of the body, like blood pressure, heartbeat, and pain, I could not help wondering about his ignorance. Was there something about the American male executive, overworked or work-obsessed, that gradually narrowed his range of interests? Was this another example of why, in recent years and especially in Rochester, I had begun to find women more interesting to talk with?

Unless assigned as a journalist to the topic, it would no more have occurred to me to sign up for a TM or mind-control course than to chant mantras. I was genuinely astonished, then, that two apparently superstraight businessmen like David Stirling and Harold Yanowitch had taken such a radical step. It was as if I had been told that Abe Beame was dropping acid.

Even more peculiar, I thought, was their impulse to proselytize. It was true David thought of his employees as his property, but this was the oddest version of corporate paternalism I had ever heard about. Didn't Jerry agree?

Jerry's initial reaction that day in the car was to shrug the whole thing off. Harold and David's flirtation with mind-

control would probably come and go as quickly as the Nehru
suit. But I was frankly fascinated by the psychology of these
two men who, after all, played such a central role in our lives.
Jerry, it seemed, was no longer capable of my kind of abstract
curiosity about their personalities. To me Harold and David
were like characters in a novel. To Jerry they were horribly
real, a menace to himself, the company, and those who had
staked their careers and money on them. What was obsessing
Jerry now were such mundane realities as the accounts receivable and Homex's soon-to-be-announced second-quarter
earnings. But his assumption that mind-control would have
no effect on his business life was erroneous.

During the latter part of January and all of February, it
began to look as though the business of Stirling Homex was
selling alpha waves. Only days after the death of Father
Stirling, David hired a full-time, José Silva mind-control instructor from New York, installed him in Rochester, and
systematically set about converting his one thousand employees.
Reaction within Homex to this extra-health benefit at company expense ranged from open disgust to admiration for
David's innovative spirit. Locally, newspaper reporters, getting wind of the story, speculated that here was a socially
enlightened step in employer-employee relations, and que-
ried Xerox and Kodak executives as to whether they were
offering similar courses.
Jerry's initial disinterest quickly changed to personal outrage as he began to observe the time and money being spent
to coerce employees to sign up for mind-control weekends,
which ran from six to midnight on Fridays, and from nine
A.M. to midnight all of Saturday and Sunday. As Alice said of
her adventures in Wonderland, Jerry's life at Homex became
"curiouser and curiouser," and every night he would come
home with fresh twists to the story.
David's bathroom was reputedly being refurbished to facil-
itate private meditation. Graduates of the weekend sessions
were now being told to attend weekly, evening brush-up

classes. Executives were being urged to close their doors and take morning and afternoon meditation breaks. A white-framed bulletin board was installed in Jerry's office. He was supposed to pin up on it a business problem, stare intensely at the board, and then wait for the solution to present itself like an aura.

At first Jerry and I agreed it sounded crazy, as if General Motors had suddenly insisted its employees convert to Islam, pray to Allah, installed prayer rugs, imported a Grand Mufti, and established a company mosque in order to boost morale and reverse a slump in car sales. But no one could quite bring himself to say that David Stirling had lost his marbles. Eccentric, yes. But there was also some speculation that David was crazy like a fox, that while certain people were sniggering, David was laying the groundwork for his next million—a national network of mind-control schools to rival Silva's Institute of Psychorientology.

Even Harold's psychiatrist friends, confronted by the spectacle of a middle-aged millionaire receiving private yoga instruction and meditating four times a day, reserved judgment. It might be a bit weird, but after all, Harold was no mixed-up teen-ager "into" astrology and the occult. If it worked for him, it was okay. The king was still perceived in his infallible mantle, fully clothed.

A few men at Homex flatly refused to have anything to do with mind-control. Bill Stirling—to his credit—was one. Paul Kuvecke, the young treasurer Jerry had been telling me about, was another. Jerry held out until he was more or less told by one of David's gofers that to do so would be to place oneself on the great man's shit list. Since Jerry knew he and David would soon be crossing swords on more serious matters, he decided not to argue. Besides, by now, even Jerry had become faintly curious. This was partly due to me, because if Jerry had been a sucker for instant-housing, I had become tantalized by the notion of instant self-improvement.

So while Jerry and I equally mistrusted David's motivations for pushing mind-control, the fact was I found myself eager to take the course, which was being offered to both husbands and wives. I imagined Jerry's antipathy versus my eagerness reflected profounder differences in our temperaments—the conservative versus the free spirit; the lawyer versus the artist. But I was wrong. As I later discovered, my attraction to mind-control reflected my weakness for shortcuts. Instead of a ten-day crash diet, I was looking for a forty-eight-hour personality change. Maybe I *could* learn to stop smoking, eat less, write faster, avoid depression, build self-confidence, and, yes, unleash my dormant greatness by tuning into those magical-mystery alpha waves. If it had worked for Gurdjieff and Gandhi, why not me? What did I have to lose except a mind and body that were probably functioning at half their capacity? I think, too, since the unexpected results of our "trust walk," which was, after all, a nonintellectual vehicle for emotional authenticity, I was more receptive to the promises of mind-body oneness than I might normally have been. So it was with a mixed sense of absurdity and curiosity that I sent Jerry off, one weekend in late January, to mind-control school with a pillow and blanket. Jerry felt more like a child humoring his parents.

Husbands and wives were encouraged to attend together, although the non-Homex family member paid the normal one hundred fifty dollar fee. But we decided, to avoid both spending a fortune on baby-sitters and prejudicing each other's reactions, to take the course separately.

I invited my sister up for the weekend during Jerry's initiation rite. I was eager for companionship but also eager to share her insights into whatever Jerry's reaction might be. Oddly enough, as the weekend progressed, we were amazed to find Jerry shedding his skepticism. There were mental exercises, he explained, for putting oneself to sleep, for waking oneself up without an alarm clock, for getting rid of headaches, and warding off fatigue, all of which Jerry believed might be useful. But for an articulate man, he was remarkably incoherent about the substance of the experience. It was as if he had walked out of a Reichian orgone box. It made sense when you were in it, but rational description was impossible. Above all, Jerry enjoyed the camaraderie of the class. It was the closest he would ever come to realizing the good fantasies he had once had of the Homex esprit. But he had been neither transformed nor turned off. One afternoon he did, for the first time in his life, manage to nap while the children were yelping and screaming through the house. But I detected no more profound effect. I would have to judge the experience myself. The second weekend in February I did.

Homex's mind-control school had been set up in another one of David's white elephants—office space in an industrial park that had been rented, lavishly decorated in anticipation of the imminent boom in business, then left unoccupied when sales dropped. The company had been trying to sublet the property for months, but now its wall-to-wall carpeted rooms became a perfect setting for a learning process that took place, as in a natural childbirth class, largely on one's back.

There were between twenty and thirty novitiates in my group. Our teacher was the venerable A. Gerald Merklinger, Piscean, ex-football player, and cosmetics salesman, now pitching a new line of goods. Merklinger, thirty years old, was as spiritual in appearance as Charles Bronson. His most disarming trait, in fact, was his apparent normalcy. This was no saffron-robed kook.

The pattern of the sessions was quickly established. Merklinger delivered long preambles about what we were about to learn, interwoven with an informal history of ESP, psychic phenomena, mind-control, believe-it-or-not-tales of mental telepathy, communication with the dead, and cancer remissions. I understood why Jerry had not been able to recapture Merklinger's monologues because, although they had been carefully structured to hold one's interest, they were a sophisticatedformofrevivalism.

After this "lecture," Merklinger would teach us how to reach our alpha levels where we would remain, in a darkened room, listening to a tape of electronic noise and the hypnotic tick of a metronome, for about fifteen minutes. These "conditionings" were very pleasant. Instead of forced labor, they were forced rest. As we reclined "in alpha," psychic messages were dished out like cups of bouillon to supine passengers on a mental trip. We were in a "deeper, healthier level of mind." We were to concentrate on such positive thoughts as, "Every day in every way I am getting better and better." (Score one for Norman Vincent Peale.) "My increasing mental faculties are for serving humanity better." (Let's hear it for Albert Schweitzer.) "Positive thoughts bring me benefits and advantages I desire." (Like money, power, and sex.) "I have full control and complete dominion over my senses and faculties at this level of the mind, and at any level of the mind, including the outer conscious level." (I am not being brainwashed.)

The appalling thing was that, of course, after dozens of semiconscious catnaps, everyone did "feel fine and in perfect health, feeling better than ever before." It was as though a roomful of insomniacs had just experienced their first full night of sleep. After several of these "conditionings" I walked around the room like a roving reporter after the resurrection. An inquiring mind was not exactly welcomed.

I was profoundly disappointed. Only the most uncritical or deeply dissatisfied human being, I felt, could take this seriously. It seemed tailor-made for life's losers. But David Stirling was not a loser, yet he was mind-control's most fervent disciple. Why?

At the height of his infatuation with MC, it could be argued that David Stirling felt himself at the edge of the precipice. His father had just died and whether he admitted it or not, he was in the process of losing his company. MC offered him solace in a form that allowed him to retain his notions of superiority and God-like powers. Men of power are peculiarly susceptible to delusions of grandeur. They think of themselves as superior beings with quasi-magical gifts, and since, in our society, egocentricity and self-confidence are considered prerequisites for human achievement, men who possess more than their share—the Nixons and Kissingers—are rarely regarded as demented. Not when they are winning. But there is a crucial difference between the man who is self-confident and the man who believes himself omnipotent.

During the second day of my mind-control weekend Merklinger related another one of his stories, this one about a child with ESP who had outsmarted a platoon of geological engineers by mentally locating underground oil fields where none were thought to exist. It was the kind of tale he had told dozens of times in different ways, but on this occasion a Homex engineer, whose very job it was to evaluate land sites before construction, rose to his feet, outraged.

"Are you saying, Mr. Merklinger, that if I went to David Stirling and told him I had mentally discovered a swamp where we had planned to build our high rise, he wouldn't laugh me out of his office?"

Merklinger replied, "If you think your boss would laugh, then I don't think you understand him very well."

The room became totally quiet. Then Merklinger added, obviously wrestling with how much he could reveal, "David Stirling is already employing some of Homex's most psychic graduates for just such purposes."

During the next coffee break, following an intuition, I approached a secretary who had become something of a MC addict. Very matter of factly I said, "I suppose David has been communing with his father since his death."

"Oh yes," she replied, smiling reverently. "He talks to him every day."

Pushing a bit further I inquired whether *she* was one of Merklinger's star pupils, devoting her psychic powers to David's business problems. Torn between pride and what must have been a vow of secrecy, she hesitated, then nodded, and I turned away.

At that moment, the fun went out of the games. During the final call to the "energy circle," I felt like a renegade camper singing, "Friends, friends, friends . . ." who can't wait to get the hell out.

Jerry and I had spent many hours after our "trust walk" discussing the unrealistic behavior of David and Harold.

There was something fundamentally inexplicable in their continued optimism and extravagance. When I had first speculated about their conversion to mind-control, I had assumed that, contrary to appearances, there was a hunger in these men that went beyond wealth and power. They might be greedy, cynical, corrupt, and ruthless, but their yearning for inner peace, for mind-body oneness was a small, redemptive quality to be honored, no matter how misguided it might turn out to be. Now that the last piece in this strange jigsaw puzzle had fallen into place, I realized the sentimentality of my perspective.

The financial deterioration of the company proceeded unchecked during January and February of 1972. The assembly line continued to hum. Thousands of dollars were poured into Merklinger's mind-control school. David and Harold jetted off, with families, for a European ski trip, and no substantial new business was coming in. Close to ten thousand modules were stashed away in locations throughout the Northeast, all theoretically "sold," but most of which were assigned to projects that would never be built. Many were crumbling from months and often years of exposure to weather. Although there was no public announcement, Homex was trying to get out of its high-rise contract with HUD since they could not afford to build at the price they had agreed to. Its "wet core" construction idea had proved as soggy as I had predicted, and while a new, $55 million loan agreement with the banks had been negotiated, the terms now included pledging the uninstalled modules as security. The banks had also demanded a reduction of inventory. Yet David and Harold continued to believe that Homex's second-quarter earnings, based on sales up to January 31 and to be published no later than March 15, would show a sizable profit. But Jerry, Paul Kuvecke, and vice-president/secretary Emil Bartz, who a decade before had lived through the bankruptcy of William Zeckendorf's real-estate empire, did not.

Jerry and I now talked about Homex's financial situation daily. It was as though we were co-authors of a mystery novel. We were closer than we had ever been, and although for

Jerry it was a tragic drama, for me, I was at last sharing the central drama of my husband's life.

Since the industrial revolution when men went off to work and women stayed home, women have traditionally lived in the world vicariously, through their husbands. They have upheld moral virtues in the house and often tried to exert moral standards on their husbands' business relationships. The traditional role of woman as moral refiner often backfires, as in the case of Martha Mitchell, whose tacky honesty was viewed as both a threat and a form of disloyalty by her husband. But now Jerry and I saw ourselves as two honorable people caught up in a corporate world where to apply standards of probity one would teach one's children was to be considered mad.

It was part of Jerry's responsibility as a lawyer, and as the company's securities expert, to file quarterly the statement of earnings—known as a Form 10-Q. But Jerry had concluded that a large portion of Homex's so-called receivables, listed as assets on its balance sheet, were a sham. The truth was that probably 40 percent of those modules would never be sold.

Whenever Jerry tried to scrutinize the facts and figures upon which the upcoming 10-Q would be based, Harold told him in effect, it was none of his business. But Jerry knew the SEC could charge him with fraud if, subsequently, the statements were discovered to be false. Blind, unquestioning obedience was no longer an option. And it was while he was wrestling with alternate options—to quit, to confront Harold and David with his suspicions, to refuse to send off the 10-Q and be fired—that David precipitated Jerry's decision by a desperate and foolhardy act.

David sent out a press release announcing a $21 million contract for a housing project to be known as Patio Homes. To Jerry it was something cooked up to massage second-quarter earnings. In fact, the contract was not signed.

Kuvecke, as treasurer, refused to go along with the scheme. Moreover, it frightened him sufficiently to agree with Jerry's decision to openly challenge the upcoming financial statement. All that remained was to gather the facts, honestly appraise the accounts receivable, and confront David and Harold with a true picture of earnings.

Paul Kuvecke, Jerry, and Emil Bartz moved cautiously, surreptitiously, and after hours. Kuvecke possessed a list of the purported accounts receivable, but had no way of judging its veracity. Jerry, knowing the men responsible for each project, gingerly and informally inquired as to the status of each project. Together, they pieced together the dismal picture.

During the last week in February Jerry wrote and rewrote a top-secret memorandum to David Stirling, Harold Yanowitch, and William Stirling on the company's financial reporting. It was a three-page bombshell whose dry, legal language belied the years of personal misery and soul-searching that had precipitated its creation. When Jerry finished the final draft he showed it to me, much as I had showed him my articles before sending them out. It seemed, in truth, a puny, passionless thing, and yet it was all there, an honorable, honest document at last.

It began quietly enough:

> The Company will shortly file a Form 10-Q with the Securities and Exchange Commission containing the quarterly results for the period ending January 31, 1972. Concurrently, we will be presenting our financial statements in the Offering Circular to be used in connection with the sale of bonds from the Mississippi plant. With the promulgation of those figures imminent, I think it appropriate to set forth certain matters for management's consideration. It is suggested that in the light of the Company's experience over the past several years, substantial adjustment is necessary in those financial statements to accurately reflect the financial condition of the Company. We need not belabor the consequences of issuing a report which contains material misstatements or omits to state material facts.

There followed a list of nine projects—adding up to between $25 and $40 million, which Jerry suggested would never be collected, and against which a reserve (or paper debit) be established. Jerry's first example of uncollectible receivables conveys the memo's tone:

> We carry a receivable of approximately $9½ million for the sale of modules to the Mississippi nonprofit corporation. This receivable in large part is approximately twelve months old. Since not a single house has been built nor a dollar collected, it is reasonable to assume that the financial ability of the customer to pay is in doubt. Is it not a fact that there is no firm long-term financing?

Jerry made clear his motivation for writing this memorandum in his closing paragraph.

> The liabilities which may arise if the financial statements are subsequently found to be wanting are not limited to the members of senior management, but to other participants within the Company who knowingly assisted in the preparation of statements and reports which do not comply with the standards required under the Securities law. These would include, in addition to members of the Executive Committee, at least the senior vice-president, treasurer, and controller.

Finally, after suggesting "the statements can be made more accurate and that the Company and its employees will be the healthier for it," Jerry added, "Messrs. Kuvecke and Bartz concur in the conclusions set forth."

Jerry hoped the memo would trigger a variety of steps. First, a realistic second-quarter earnings statement showing a sizable loss. This would kill the stock but perhaps save the company. Second, a bank-precipitated change in management, with Kuvecke and Dienstag on top or, at least, Stirling and Yanowitch removed. I was skeptical of this latter possibility. Only in Hollywood are palace revolutions successful. In real life the good guys lose their jobs and are lucky if they can pay the mortgages on their houses. I thought it more likely Jerry would be fired, and frankly, after two and a half years of watching my husband turn into a haggard, silent, business stiff, I prayed he would be. I craved a final and dramatic

denouement. I wanted Jerry to have only one choice left—
to find a new job, to face himself, to evaluate, once and for
all, the relationship between work and family, the real price
to be paid for financial success and upward mobility in
American society.

The reality of losing the house, of my going back to a
full-time job, of Jerry taking a drastic cut in pay for work he
enjoyed, did not frighten me. Romantic to the core, I welcomed it. Although Jerry was a decent, honorable man—the
kind of person every TV show, every comic book, every
movie and newspaper editorial tells us we should be—I was
beginning to wonder whether American corporatism was
not, by its compulsion to show ever-increasing profits, by its
unhealthy relationship to the rise and fall of the stock market,
morally flawed at its core. Was it possible to be a successful
businessman and still retain a moral conscience?

I now saw Jerry as the white knight, the man of integrity
riding off to battle. And yet he was an ordinary man, like the
old-fashioned honest cop. I was very proud. I felt a part of his
moral actions but most of all, it was a mutual moral victory.

All middle-class women, comfortable women with houses
and two cars and enough leisure time to "find themselves"
creatively or "lose themselves" destructively, wonder if they
have not violated their integrity as easily and completely as
their husbands. Wives who piously tell their children not to
steal from Woolworth's have few qualms about their husbands padding bills on the expense account. Honesty in marriage, as well as in business, involves a view of life as a moral
wholeness. Few couples are ever directly confronted with a
challenge to their moral smugness. We had been and experienced an incredible sense of joy at surmounting that
challenge in an honorable way. I was at peace with myself.
We were at peace with each other. On the morning of leap
year day, February 29, as Jerry departed for work to deliver
the memo, we sat at the breakfast table enveloped by an
almost sexual intimacy. We had become again each other's
hero and friend. Echoing my deepest fantasies, Jerry
quipped, as he went out the door, "See you at OK Corral."

Fall 1972

CHAPTER XII

Eight months later, on a Monday afternoon in early October, the phone rang. It was my friend and uprooted comrade Marge Rosen, whose husband had been the former chief site-planner for Homex.

"I presume you've seen the evening paper," she said in a curiously portentous voice.

"No," I replied. "I've been in my office working all day. What's up?"

"Oh." There was a slight pause. "I was sure you'd have heard by now. It's Jerry. His name is all over the front page of *The Times Union.*

"My God, why?" I lowered myself onto the edge of the bed.

"Well, the Homex bankruptcy hearings began today. It seems the trustee is using a memo Jerry wrote to attack the credibility of the Stirlings."

"The memorandum? They found the memorandum?" I didn't believe it, since the Stirlings and Yanowitch had supposedly destroyed their copies and Jerry, refusing to turn his over, had put his in a safe-deposit box. It seemed incredible that such a damning bit of evidence had been left behind. But they had bungled so many other things, why not this too?

Marge read me the headline and lead paragraph:

STIRLING QUIZ
OPENS: FOCUS
PUT ON MEMO

Stirling Homex Corp.'s trustee today brought forth a document he said was a memorandum suggesting that $25 million in reserves be set up to cover "accounts receivable" that might not be collectible.

"Yes, that's it all right," I said, exultant. She read on:

The trustee, Frank G. Raichle, described the memorandum as he quizzed David Stirling, Jr., the first witness in his investigation of the collapse of the Avon manufacturer of modular housing.

Stirling was Chairman of the Board of the company until his resignation just before it filed bankruptcy proceedings in July.

The memorandum, dated February 29, 1972, was signed by Jerome Dienstag, then an assistant vice-president and associate general counsel at Stirling Homex. He later left the company.

Dienstag said that Paul Kuvecke, vice-president for finance who later became president, and Emil Bartz, vice-president and secretary, concurred in his conclusions.

The three-page memorandum appeared to be a big gun in a developing Raichle position that Stirling Homex Corp. had used unsound practices in recording and reporting its financial position.

Jerry had gone out of town for a two-day business conference with his new corporate employer. It occurred to me I'd better get hold of him quickly before some stranger surprised him with the news. I cut Marge's reading short, rushed downstairs to see if our evening paper had been delivered, which it had, and quickly glanced at the six-column story before dialing the Sheraton Hotel in Canandaigua. By chance, Jerry was in his room, changing before dinner, when I rang.

"Jerry, you're not going to believe this, but Raichle found your memo. It's the first thing he threw at David this morning when he got on the witness stand. It's all in the evening papers. I'm afraid your days of anonymity are over."

Jerry's reaction, as I had foreseen, was not one of unmitigated joy. Lawyers are a guarded bunch. While I suspected that ultimately Jerry would enjoy the limelight, I knew his first concern would be to protect his privacy and ascertain to what extent it had already been invaded. I read aloud the entire account of the day's hearings. It contained only one peculiar exchange, tucked away in the next-to-the-last column. "Raichle asked whether he had threatened to fire Dienstag, and Stirling answered, 'I never threatened to fire anyone.' "

We both knew that was true, and we wondered who had suggested otherwise. In fact, not only had David made no overt move against Jerry, he never even discussed the memorandum with him. Instead, the confrontation had taken place between Jerry and Harold. But all of this had been a private drama. Whatever the suspicions of our Rochester friends, Jerry's resignation from Homex in late May was explained as a routine switch to a better job. And when in July the company's bankruptcy rocked the community, we remained silent. Now this sudden turn of events meant that what we believed was a closed chapter in our lives would be reopened. Our private nightmare would become a public spectacle. Although Jerry's reputation could only be enhanced by the facts, I knew that whatever pleasure we might take in subsequent revelations would be equaled by the pain of reliving them.

In the end, Jerry's luck had held, although I did not believe it would at the time. To me, of all the postmemorandum scenarios I had envisaged, the least desirable one had happened. Nothing had happened. The gunfight had come to nothing. Although Harold had charged into Jerry's office accusing him of disloyalty, and Jerry had angrily retorted, "My job is to be loyal to the company, not to the Stirlings," Harold's only response was, "Well, David runs this company," and that seemed to be that. Jerry was not fired; he was simply treated as a leper, a nonperson by the Stirlings and Yano- witch from then on. Superficially, Jerry's office life went on as usual, but in fact Jerry was given no serious work, and he spent his days in a weird limbo, shuffling papers and reading *The Wall Street Journal* from cover to cover.

By now I was totally exasperated with Jerry's behavior. He had made his move and then again turned passive. I began to fear he was capable of doing nothing forever. He con- tinued to confer with Kuvecke and still clung to the hope that a coup d'état was imminent, but he refused to look for a new job.

In March, perhaps due to Jerry's memo, a curtain was partially raised on Homex's faltering financial situation. The company reported a $2 million loss for the previous quarter. How the figure of $2 million had been arrived at was another mystery. Perhaps it was believed that investors could live with a $2 million loss and not panic. But they guessed wrong. For an overhyped, under-financed company whose stock market value was almost totally based on promises of fantas- tic future earnings, the revelation was catastrophic.

The stock began to plummet. Merrill Lynch backed out of the Mississippi bond offering. The dream of a new plant gen- erating $100 million in business was over. And when it was publicly announced that the "Operation Breakthrough" con- tract had been terminated, the high-rise fantasy was also over. From then on, throughout April and May, the company was deluged with phone calls from distraught investors many of whom turned out to be the proverbial "widows and or- phans." Jerry's reward for not quitting was to find that Har- old directed these phone calls to him—the SEC expert.

Night after night Jerry came home with terrible tales. A mother had sunk her entire fortune into Homex. What should she do now? A man had counted on Homex stock for his retirement. How, I wondered, could Jerry stand it? What would it take to bomb him out of that office? I felt helpless against his passivity and terribly angry. I hounded him constantly—at home, in the psychiatrist's office, none of which helped our marriage or increased my respect. I was open about my feelings. I did not hide them like a good little wife, but my implorations accomplished nothing, except to reopen wounds. Had he written his résumé yet? I would find his last one and help update it. Jerry couldn't bring himself to even look at it. Had he called any of his lawyer friends in New York? Not yet. He didn't know what to say. Had he put an ad in *The Wall Street Journal?* Had he answered any of *The New York Times* ads I had assiduously clipped from the Sunday paper? And why was I doing the damn clipping? But it was no use. I would find the ads stuffed under the cushions of the couch or mysteriously "lost." It was as though I were asking Jerry to write his death warrant. Here was a man who possessed extraordinary powers of imagination and energy when faced with legal or administrative problems, but who confronted his future like a terrified child in a rudderless ship.

Finally, after weeks of hounding, Jerry made a few tentative moves. He placed a blind ad in *The Wall Street Journal* and called several friends. But the results were depressing. The ad only brought letters of inquiry from headhunters, and New York, as we knew, was in the midst of a recession. Law firms were firing securities experts.

It looked as if we were in for a long and terrible process of knocking on doors, of dispirited interviews, of being told one was underqualified or overqualified, too old or too young, of fruitless flights to Washington and New York, of waiting for letters that never came or hearing of jobs that had just been filled.

Jerry still refused to breathe a word of his distress to anyone in Rochester. I abided by his decision partly because I still hoped to get the hell out, but partly because I agreed that the risk of being fired was not worth taking. The rules made no sense but we both understood that prospective employers prefer to hire a man who appears secure and unhurriedly looking around, than one who is unemployed and desperate. I had no idea how employers regarded men associated with bankrupt companies, but given Jerry's nature and the country's depressed economy, I believed Jerry would only swim for his life when the company finally went under.

On April 13, I turned thirty-four. Even in the best of times I do not take birthdays with equanimity, less because of advancing age than because all "special occasions" provoke in me fantasies of perfect pleasure—of the right present delivered at the right moment by the unexpectedly right person —that can never be fulfilled. Like any child, I yearn to be pampered and indulged. Thoroughly embarrassed by such feelings, I pretend indifference and secretly wallow in self-pity. As a husband, Jerry was uniquely unsuited to my fantasy of inspired gift-giver. His mother believed frivolous presents an indulgence and often used birthdays as occasions to present a pair of pajamas or socks. My mother, a child herself, turned birthdays into moments of magic. I knew, by now, Jerry would, after numerous reminders and plaintive inquiries as to "What I wanted," at the last moment buy a night-gown and consider himself relieved of further celebrative gestures. I knew I would be disappointed, and every year I vowed to avoid the emotional trap I had ingeniously set for myself. But on my thirty-fourth birthday I didn't even try to pretend I was happy. I had good reason to be depressed. It was what I had come to call slit-your-wrists weather: rainy, cold, remorselessly gray. Jerry was still gripped by a paralysis of will, and while I had successfully jumped from suburban journalism to cover stories for *Upstate*, it appeared likely that my triumph would be short-lived, that in six months I would find myself in some new town, with no contacts, no friends, no job, having to begin all over again.

I was in some respects a solitary person, and prided myself on the degree to which I could remain sane and productive living a monastic life at the typewriter. But not being able to talk to anyone about the uncertainty of the future was, by now, compounding the agony. Finally I experienced an overwhelming desire to talk, to confide, to make a real connection with another human being. I couldn't concentrate on my work. It was too late to make a lunch date. I had combed every museum in town and didn't know what to do with myself. In New York I might have treated myself to an afternoon movie, but Rochester did not provide such matinée solace for distraught wives. So, on an impulse, late in the afternoon, I dropped in at an art gallery run by a woman whose enthusiasm for life I hoped would cheer me up. It was a chance encounter that turned out to be the closest thing to the right present at the right moment I will probably ever experience.

My friend happened to be in an equally uncertain period of her life. In a burst of intimacy she revealed to me her decision to sell the gallery and I, needing little encouragement, revealed our predicament, including Jerry's job dissatisfaction and the difficulty, in a small town, of looking around for something else. My friend immediately understood the nature and complexity of this kind of family crisis. A generation older, the wife of a corporate executive and mother of grown children, she had always pursued a separate career and lived through the ups and downs of her husband's career. Her intense sympathy was a comfort and relief. Somehow it was important to know that a woman I respected had been through it all and survived. It occurred to me, as we were talking, that this sort of confession between women was what rap sessions were all about. They filled a need once met by generations of women within a single family, but which, with families scattered and the goals of women so diverse, could no longer be handled by mothers and grandmothers. If one were lucky one found female surrogates. That day I was very lucky.

My friend had met Jerry only once or twice at art openings. They had liked each other immediately, but she had not the slightest idea what he did for a living or even where he worked. We chatted for about an hour, about Jerry's job and background, about my work for *Upstate,* about what we both thought we'd be doing in a year, and I left the gallery feeling inexplicably gay, as though I had bought a new dress. Astonishingly, that hour of conversation produced the miracle

Jerry had been waiting for. The woman's husband, as I knew but had not thought much about, was chairman of the board of a prominent local company. It seemed his company had been searching for a lawyer with Jerry's precise corporate and securities qualifications for months. That evening just as I was telling Jerry about my afternoon, my friend's husband called. Within a few weeks Jerry was offered the job.

It seemed an irony beyond all ironies that I should provide the means for our remaining in Rochester. It was like stabbing myself in the back. But once I had gotten over the shock, I began to think that, like characters in a melodrama, we were being given a second chance to relive a crisis that had brought us such pain three years before.

Our discussions about moving or staying bore little resemblance to the ones that had taken place—or failed to take place—the first time around. Jerry's career was only part of the picture. The other equal parts were what was best for me, for my career, for our children, and for our marriage. It was less a question of a great opportunity for Jerry—although it might prove to be one—than whether our mutual needs could be met in this city. It had taken us fourteen years to even pose the right questions, but posing them did not guarantee we would come up with the right answers.

Jerry would never have left New York City for the position he was now being offered. Neither the job nor the company were glamorous, and its corporate offices were Dickensian. But he had lost his appetite for the glamorous executive lifestyle that was as nourishing as junk food. He craved not security but sanity—a real company whose profits were based on real sales; the full use of his talents; legal challenges he could pursue with honor. Now that was more than enough.

Three years before he had mouthed platitudes about the good family life the way politicians talk about a balanced budget. It had been a device to get me to vote for the move. It had nothing to do with the kind of people we were. We were not suburbanites who enjoyed mowing the grass and playing touch football with neighborhood children. We were intensely private adults with urban tastes, devoted to our children but not capable of revolving our lifestyle around them. Jerry now understood that being a father and husband required more than a magical move to a house and garden. The marriage could not be set like an electric clock and then ignored. It needed daily winding. It could not be his part-time hobby and my full-time responsibility. Any job that drained him, that involved impossible hours and perpetual anxiety could not be a "good" job. I did not say these things to him. He said them to me. So the opportunities and limitations of this offer at this time had to be weighed in the broader context of the kind of marriage and life we realistically envisaged as satisfying for ourselves. Jerry's priorities had profoundly changed, and mine, in a way, had changed too.

I still missed New York and still dreamt of someday going back. But I had evolved a balance between writing and the demands of domesticity that was superior to anything I had achieved before. Also, despite Jerry's conversion to a more equitable marriage, I had a more realistic view of his limitations. He was not and would never be the kind of man who enjoyed helping around the house. Now that his sons were older, he spent more time with them, but he would never leap out of bed in the morning to take them on a hike, he would never bake bread or enjoy tinkering in the basement or take to gardening or transform himself from a city mouse to a country mouse. He had changed enough to keep our marriage going, and with Jesse finally out of diapers, he was prepared, at night or on weekends, to take more responsibility for him. It occurred to him now to straighten an unmade bed. He often presided over the children's baths. He pierced the mystery of the dishwasher and, when he ran out of clean underwear, the washing machine. These were major steps in the right direction, done less out of pleasure than duty. But still I frankly feared another move. Even knowing what we did about ourselves, or perhaps knowing how unnatural, how unspontaneous it was for Jerry to concentrate his time and energy on the family, I suspected another move would put a terrible strain on that fragile balance between personal freedom and marital obligations that had been so recently achieved.

It had taken me two years to settle into a large house in a new city. The practical details of being a mother and housewife were absorbing less of my time and freeing me to do more work. Any move, even back to New York, would temporarily reverse that equation. I would have to find new baby-sitters, new schools, and again restructure my life. The thought of wrenching myself out of a perfect writing groove seemed foolhardy. Selfishly then, I was better off in Rochester. At least for the time being. It would be difficult to pursue a national free-lance career from Rochester, but not impossible. If one day in the future I decided I could not develop as a writer in this city, that contacts and opportunities open to New York-based writers were being denied me because of where I lived, then we might have to reevaluate our decision. But I could not say I had reached that point yet.

Above all, neither of us felt locked into this decision for life. Having survived the most basic of all deracinations—leaving home—future ones no longer frightened me. I had lost my New York rigidity. I could live in the provinces without becoming provincial. Although my passion for New York had not abated, my relationship to it had undergone a subtle change, from total dependency to what, in another context, has come to be known as open marriage.

On balance, then, there seemed no logical reason for uprooting again, especially given Jerry's passivity about job hunting. Jerry would take the job and begin work June 15.

The mutuality of the decision freed us from feeling we were in Rochester for the wrong reasons. Jerry no longer felt chained to a job and I no longer felt like a camp follower. Psychologically we had moved to commit ourselves to our new life. It was as if, after two years of temporary residence, we were ready to file citizenship papers.

When we wrote to various New York friends about Jerry's resignation and our decision to remain in Rochester, the collective wave of incredulity that greeted us made me realize just how profoundly we had changed in so short a time. Our ordeal had taught us where our natural talents lay and what kind of work gave us real pleasure as distinct from money and prestige. Despite his false start at Homex, Jerry discovered he preferred working for a corporation to a private practice. He was, it turned out, a fine administrator and he enjoyed the variety of corporate and legal problems that came across his desk. Despite my false starts I had come to prefer the freedom of free-lance feature writing to the security of a job or the narrowness of a journalist's beat. We both believed we could develop our careers in Rochester as well as anywhere and, given the recent shakiness of our marriage, a spell of normalcy would quicken the healing process.

Oddly enough, only weeks after Jerry's resignation, the coup d'état he had long envisaged at Homex took place. The banks insisted Kuvecke replace Bill Stirling as president, and on June 15, just as Jerry began his new job, Kuvecke had the unique pleasure of announcing at a board meeting that Homex's losses for the first three quarters of the fiscal year were almost $20 million. Employees began being fired in weekly waves. On June 14 the Stirlings and Yanowitch were forced to resign. But it was all too late. The banks refused to extend their loans and demanded repayment of the outstanding $38 million. On July 7, the company ran out of money and officially declared bankruptcy.

The effect of Homex's bankruptcy far exceeded the actual loss of one thousand jobs. Rochesterians had heavily invested in what they had been led to believe was "the Xerox of the seventies." Many analysts had touted the stock to the very end. No one had been prepared for the sudden collapse, and there was a persistent mood of outrage and betrayal. How could such a thing have happened so swiftly and without warning? How could so many stockbrokers have been fooled for so long? Had information been withheld? Had there been an inside conspiracy of silence? Had the banks cleverly secured their loans four months and seventeen days prior to forcing the company into bankruptcy, thereby leaving other creditors out in the cold? The list of unanswered questions kept rumors flying and newspaper reporters digging.

As Homex went through its public death-throes, we were quietly celebrating our return to an ordinary existence. Jerry took a two-week vacation between jobs, a week of which was spent on a family trip to New York. As if to underscore the changes that had taken place in our marriage, it was Jerry who visited with friends and shuttled the children between grandparents while I made the rounds of editors' offices like an actress on the comeback trail. Armed with three pages of article ideas and a portfolio of recent work I set off each morning with ingénue freshness and staggered back to my parents' apartment each evening wondering if my ambitions were worth facing the remarkable indifference of editors to my talent. But the ordeal paid off. I secured an agent, and in that serendipitous fashion that is the only constant in a free-lancer's life, received an assignment from *Ms.* magazine on the personal adventures of an uprooted wife. It would not, I admit, have occurred to me that my recent ordeal was of universal interest, but an editor at *Ms.*, after casually chatting with me about where I was living and why, immediately recognized that the subject, as told from the woman's point of view, was virgin territory. Other contacts initiated that week slowly produced further assignments as the months wore on. I had never had a more productive or happier summer.

I approached the writing of the *Ms.* piece with great trepidation. Although it was mainly about me and our marriage, and very peripherally about Stirling Homex, it meant candidly discussing our recent domestic crisis. Jerry, to my great pride, was neither alarmed nor threatened by what I might say. And what I did reveal, about moving for the wrong reasons, about failing to confront the implications of the move, about his initial failure as a husband after the move, was not very complimentary. But writing the article had the unforeseen effect of bringing Jerry and me even closer together. It was a good and challenging piece of work because I learned more about myself and my husband through setting down in words the series of traumas that had befallen us. It deepened our perceptions of what had gone wrong, and with hindsight, certain logical and universally relevant observations could be made that would be of help to other women about to face a similar predicament.

Noticeably absent, too, was the strain that had often accompanied Jerry's editorial opinions about my work. He had always functioned as my first reader, but until that article I had frequently distrusted his judgment. But either because Jerry was a member of the dramatis personae in this play or because I had reached that point of confidence where I could regard my writing with greater objectivity, there was not the slightest dissension between us on my handling of the piece. So it was with a double sense of pride and accomplishment that I learned of its acceptance. It seemed a fitting coda to what I believed were the symphonic complexities of the past two years.

The article appeared in the November issue of *Ms.*, which arrived on newsstands and in mailboxes in mid-October, at the precise moment Jerry's name and face were plastered all over the morning and evening papers as the author of "the much-feared Dienstag memo." I had not, in my article, alluded to the memo or even mentioned the name of his employer. I had merely revealed that his dream job had turned into a nightmare and that he had left it for another position in Rochester. But now, of course, Rochesterians could read between the lines more than I had intended. We became for a while, and in a small way, a rather notorious couple. When I went to a department store and handed a sales lady my charge card, she took one look at my name and immediately knew who I was.

CHAPTER XIII

From October 2 to October 8 the bankruptcy hearings dominated the local news. Like everyone else Jerry and I devoured the coverage. A bankruptcy hearing is not a trial. It is an investigative procedure conducted before a federal judge, in a federal courtroom, open to the public and press,

and procedurally similar to a trial. Witnesses are under oath;
testimony is recorded by court stenographers; and rules of
evidence disputed between the trustee for the bankrupt corporation and the witnesses' lawyers. A bankruptcy hearing
can uncover indictable evidence, but cannot indict.

The job of the trustee is to represent the defunct company's best interest, to ascertain its remaining assets, to explore the feasibility of reorganization and to conduct the
postmortem with an eye to further civil suits against former
management if fraud is uncovered. In this instance the court-
appointed trustee was seventy-four-year-old Frank G.
Raichle, a formidable trial lawyer with a national reputation
who was described, by a reporter covering the hearings, as
"a piranha in court." The first three witnesses were the Stirlings and Yanowitch. Their frequent lapses of memory,
vagueness about their duties and insistence that, in Harold's
words, "Homex ran out of cash when the company was probably in its best posture. . . . in terms of installation of
modules," were treated with withering sarcasm by Raichle
who possessed a quick, humorous mind and talent for one-
line zingers. Reporters found Raichle's humor irresistible,
and I would be less than honest if I denied savoring the
public humiliation of the Stirlings and Yanowitch. As in a
classic drama, the protagonists had been brought down by
their own arrogance and I relished the justice of the retribu-
tion.

Jerry had not yet been approached by Raichle, but during
a two-week recess he was called to appear as a witness.
Raichle would put Jerry on the stand October 20.

Before that, we went to New York for a weekend. We saw
old friends and relatives who were rather spellbound by this
final twist to our tale of fame and fortune in the provinces.
My *Ms.* article had been read with varying degrees of shock.
Everyone had known of my antipathy toward the move and
Rochester, but no one had been aware of how close it had
come to destroying our marriage. My mother complimented
me on my writing style, but said not a word about the substance of my remarks. The wife of a friend said she had been

saddened to read of our distress, but no one was eager to engage me in conversation about the feminist issues I had raised. It occurred to me, finally, that they were too threatening to both husbands and wives, that while some women might agree with me and some not, it frightened couples to confront the subject of uprooted wives—especially in my presence. I later heard that dinner party arguments raged in Rochester and New York when neither of us was around. But somehow, in an age when people think nothing of discussing their sexual lives, friends were uncomfortable with intimate revelations of another order. Without meaning to, I had violated one of the last American taboos—to write honestly about the repercussions of a man's career on his marriage and values. It was a familiar subject in fiction, but stepping out from behind that protective screen, writing of my pain in the first person was, to many, bad form. Had I gotten a divorce and then written the same article, no one would have questioned my right to delineate the disintegration of a marriage since the cannibalism of ex-wives was a comfortably familiar phenomenon. But here we were, still married, obviously more devoted to one another than ever, having bared our ugliest feelings and worst moments. *That* was embarrassing. Everyone understood that marriages had their ups and downs. In the months to come I would hear innumerable private confessions from married women friends about the lows and highs of their unions. But they feared talking about it openly because—and this was the heart of the matter—they were convinced their husbands couldn't take it. This point of view was finally expressed to me openly by a woman who admired both me and my husband. "How could you have written such terrible things about Jerry?" she asked me. And to Jerry, "How could you have permitted your wife to write so frankly about your mistakes and weaknesses?" My father, it turned out, was most concerned that the article would damage Jerry's career; my friend believed the article was destructive to his male image, which is to say, that façade of strength and unflagging wisdom that for generations has been synonymous with the noun, man. No one congratulated Jerry—as they should have—for possessing an ego, a self-image strong enough to withstand the truth. He understood his frailties and was not demeaned by them or their public disclosure. My respect for him soared. If others saw him as a weak husband unable to control his wife, then their values were upside down, not ours. But since many couples devote a large portion of their lives to camouflaging their real feelings about each other from themselves and the rest of the world, I suspect they envied the honest basis of our marriage.

Notoriety was not altogether a pleasant experience, we discovered. On the one hand, the weird coincidence of my article's publication days before Jerry was to take the witness stand had dangerous ramifications. There was the distinct possibility that the *Ms.* article might be used to discredit Jerry, to make it appear his motivation for writing the memo had less to do with his job than with the state of his marriage. Jerry thought it unlikely, but I thought it highly likely, and on the day we set out for court, it was very much on my mind.

Jerry took the stand at 10:30 A.M. I knew he had not slept well and was exceedingly nervous, but he appeared relaxed, almost languorous as he waited for the questioning to begin, while I was shaking so hard I had to grip the edge of the courtroom bench to steady myself. I had never been in a courtroom before and the fear it inspired in me was a revelation. Jerry was "one of the good guys," and he had nothing to hide, but somehow the profound seriousness of the setting, the public and irreversible nature of the proceedings coupled with the possibility of my article being used as a weapon against my husband, frightened the hell out of me.

The morning's testimony brought no surprises. Raichle asked Jerry the obvious questions—why he had written the memo, from whom he had gathered the facts—and gradually I relaxed. But he was still in the midst of his interrogation when the decision was made to break for lunch. The cross-examination was still to come, and although Jerry insisted he was not apprehensive, I could tell that he was all wound up. Exuberant and expansive, we sat down to lunch alone.

One of the least understandable aspects of our so-called notoriety was the conspicuous ring of silence from both personal and business friends. It had occurred to me that while, in theory, society applauds an honest lawyer, nobody really likes a Mr. Clean, which was the way Jerry looked in newspaper and magazine stories about the bankruptcy. We hadn't been surprised not to receive an avalanche of telegrams congratulating Jerry on his probity. In fact, I had turned it into a family joke. "Well, I don't hear the phone ringing with all those big companies dying to get an honest, earnest lawyer on their team." We had both laughed, but it was one thing not to hear from General Motors and quite another not to hear from friends.

The disparity between strangers going out of their way to shake Jerry's hand and intimates not lifting up the phone to say anything was something I didn't understand. Of course, many of our friends had been introduced to us through the Yanowitches. Perhaps they were paralyzed by conflicting loyalties. And as for Jerry's ex-colleagues at Homex, perhaps they resented his coming out of the debacle unblemished. Perhaps, too, they were thinking, "That sonofabitch. If he looks like the white knight, what does that make the rest of us look like?"

But the result of the hearings, the publicity, and the phone that never rang was to reinforce our communication as husband and wife. We had so much to talk about and no one to talk about it with, except each other, and after thirteen years of marriage it was delightful to have too much rather than too little to say.

The afternoon cross-examination of Jerry was remarkably ineffective.

"Did you ever take a course in accounting?"

"No, sir," said Jerry.

"Did you ever read any literature on accounting?"

"No, sir."

"Did you ever have occasion to read any literature with respect to the percentage of completion, the accounting principle for reporting accounts receivable?"

"No."

"Did you ever run a business in the furnishing of housing of the nature and kind of Stirling Homex?"

"He never ran one into the ground!" Raichle interjected.

The courtroom howled. Reporters couldn't resist including that exchange in their stories. As far as I was concerned, the afternoon was a total rout.

During a courtroom recess, Jerry and I chatted with the only remaining lawyer at Homex, who had been sitting and taking notes all day. We were mystified as to why he was still with the company. He was a young man with a fine reputation, and of all the lawyers we knew, least encumbered by children, a house, or debts. Although it was not like Jerry to probe, he finally said, "Why don't you take your wife and go out to California?" She was from California, disliked Rochester, and once admitted to Jerry her desire to go back. The young man had no real answer. He mumbled something about having to take the California bar, and how that would be a pain in the neck, but Jerry and I suddenly understood. He was where Jerry had been six months before. He was willing to spend meaningless day after meaningless day with a moribund company rather than come to grips with the future.

The hearings were adjourned for several weeks. The Stirlings' lawyer, for reasons no one understood, insisted he would require an hour and a half more to complete his cross-examination of Jerry at that time. Although Jerry was exhausted and dismayed by the prospect of another day in court, he was also exhilarated. The hearings had affected both of us like a shot of adrenaline. That evening we couldn't stop talking about the case. We mixed ourselves a second batch of martinis. We let the children watch all the TV they wanted. We again speculated about the state of mind of Harold and Joan, like detectives obsessed by the psychology of criminals. I was still worried about my article, which had not been mentioned. But what else was left? On Thursday, November 2, we went back to court and my worst fears were confirmed.

Jerry was already seated in the witness chair when the

Stirlings' lawyer strode into the courtroom. The proceedings had not officially begun. No one was paying much attention to him except Jerry who, from his vantage point, glimpsed a magazine curled in his hand. It was the November issue of *Ms.* Jerry gestured toward the magazine for my benefit. My heart jumped. Jerry was grinning, but I felt as if in midair the motors had been cut on my plane. The lawyer marched back and forth in front of the referee, in front of Jerry, the court reporters, and Raichle, waving the magazine around, curling and uncurling it, slapping it down on his briefcase, then snatching it up as if in a paroxysm of indecision. It was a curious performance.

"I take it sir that the record indicates that Mr. Dienstag is recalled to continue his cross-examination. Mr. reporter, would you mark this for identification please." He plopped down the magazine on the court-reporter's table, like Othello waving the handkerchief for spectators in the third balcony.

The gesture had its effect. The room became quiet, everyone suddenly aware something strange was going on, this was not the normal ruffling of files and throat-clearing before getting down to business. Jerry was grinning more broadly, and gesturing at me. The reporters turned and stared; I did my best to erase the look of panic from my face. Raichle looked up and began to mutter, "What's going on?" and all eyes rested on the lawyer.

Then, in the same rambling manner in which he declared his original intention that morning to continue the cross-examination, "particularly in certain areas that I have since discovered," he suddenly announced there would be no further cross-examination. The truth had already been revealed, he said. "I have no questions."

By now, Raichle, who knew nothing about the *Ms.* article, was curious. "What is all this about? The magazine? This creates some mystery?"

"I do not wish to indulge in personal areas of the witness," the lawyer replied, with what, I thought, was a refreshing touch of dignity. Jerry was dismissed.

The hearings went on for the rest of the week with sensational revelations, even to us, of a double-bookkeeping system known to a few as "the Mickey-Mouse file" and "the real world," of perpetually reassigned modules to support the myth of audited sales, of payoffs to union officials, and illegal contributions to political coffers. As the sordid tale unfolded, Jerry looked better and better—the only genuine hero.

Jerry did not feel like a hero. He was aware how long it had taken him, as he put it at the hearings, "to stop taking orders" and of the morally ambiguous trail that had led toward the truth. But in an age when corporate immorality appeared to be the rule rather than the exception, Jerry was the closest thing to integrity one was likely to get. As Daniel Schorr later quipped about the clean-cut young men confessing their sins before the Senate Watergate hearings, "Funny thing about America, our heroes are those who confess first."

We may venerate dead heroes or, as we look backward, men who sacrificed careers in times of stress for a higher sense of personal honor. Although we would all like to believe ourselves capable of ethical behavior, the McCarthy era and, most recently, the duplicity of political and business leaders enmeshed in Watergate, have proven how few people can resist the rewards of power. The average American is awkward when confronted with moral dramas. Months after the hearings were over, I asked certain friends about their silence. Their response was twofold: "We didn't know what to say," and "We didn't want to pry." I am sure they believed it. But I am also convinced they invoked the sanctity of privacy to avoid facing their ambivalent feelings toward Jerry's behavior and momentary fame. They did not want to probe their own attitudes toward the Stirlings and Yanowitch, to admit their own attraction to quick money and the aura of success that tainted all of us. It did not occur to them we might take their silence as disapproval. As a nation we are notoriously friendly to strangers, but strangely indifferent to the needs of friends.

Epilogue 1974–1975

A federal grand jury, meeting in Rochester on December 11, 1974, returned a twenty-eight-count indictment against David Stirling, Jr., and Harold Yanowitch for allegedly violating a section of the Taft-Hartley Act that prohibits an employer from giving stock or money to labor officials. The charges are misdemeanors, with each count punishable by a year in prison or a maximum fine of ten thousand dollars or both.

In July of 1975, the Securities and Exchange Commission accused the Stirling Homex Corporation of creating phantom sales, making illegal political contributions, using illegal bugging equipment, and making payoffs to union officials. Merrill Lynch, Pierce, Fenner & Smith was named a defendant in the suit and was accused of not adequately investigating Stirling Homex's financial situation as underwriter for the preferred stock. Also named in the civil suit were David Stirling, Jr., William Stirling, and Harold Yanowitch. The SEC also criticized Peat, Marwick, Mitchell & Company for its auditing of the Stirling Homex books.

As this book goes to press in the beginning of December 1975, this is the unfinished story. There has been no final resolution in the courts to the countless civil suits.

As for Jerry, he has testified before the SEC and expects to be subpoenaed in connection with a class-action suit that has been brought against officers of the company. But emotionally his involvement is over. For a while he couldn't bear to even drive by the plant in Avon, which has been operating with a skeleton staff in order to sell off Homex's inventory, but his memory of those days is fading. His new work has proven to be the most challenging and fulfilling of his entire career, and at his fortieth-birthday party, he was the least-depressed man in the room.

A few weeks ago my son Joshua again asked me about the book I'd been working on for so long. He had recently written his autobiography for a school assignment and his curiosity had been revived as to what would be in mine. It was a cloudless spring day. We were on our way to purchase hiking boots, a canteen, and collapsible cup for his first sleep-away summer camp. He was in a happy, expansive mood, and so was I.

I explained to my son that when his father wanted to move to Rochester, I didn't want to leave New York. The book was about our move and what happened to us when we got here.

Joshua listened thoughtfully and then said, "I didn't want to leave New York either." That, of course, was not true. At the age of five he had little sense of what was happening to him, but when the familiar routines of his life were destroyed, he experienced a terrible sense of loss. It has grown into a permanent nostalgia. In his autobiography he wrote, "I started to think back. Ever since I moved to Rochester I've always wanted to move back to New York City."

Doubtless, if we returned to New York he would miss Rochester, in which he has flourished, but we had never discussed it before.

"Do you still miss New York?" Joshua asked, as everyone still does.

"Yes, I do," I replied.

"So do I," he echoed. "The thing about Rochester is that it doesn't have the best of anything. You know what I mean? It's a nice place to live but, well, it's just an average American city."

I nearly racked up the car on a telephone pole.

"I couldn't agree with you more," I said, restraining a parental urge to present both sides, to point out that we lived a far-more privileged life in Rochester than we ever could in New York. The hell with it, I decided. Why bullshit the kid.

Encouraged, my boy-genius went on. "Yeah, it doesn't have the tallest building or the most people or a major-league football team, or anything!"

Mentally, I picked up where he left off. Or variety. Or

choice. Or enough first-rate minds. Or a single French pastry shop. Or Bloomingdale's. Or adventure in the streets. Or Brentano's. Or a skyline that makes your heart stop at twilight.

But why go on? For me it holds that New York is a lover, Rochester, a husband. In New York I feel more alive, more beautiful, more passionate, more aware of the possibilities of life. Every pore is open to sensation and every sensation is there to be poured. Rochester is sturdy, comfortable, and nonthreatening. It is not only safe in the streets but also psychologically safe. The wild vicissitudes of New York careerism do not threaten one's sanity and stability in a place like Rochester. There are few stars, few flash-in-the-pans, few this year's artist who, inevitably, becomes last year's artist. In Rochester, as a writer, I compete with myself.

Rochester is a city of steady, serious workers. People come here to work, not to have fun. Nobody likes living in Rochester twelve months a year. Everyone knows it is a compromise and a very puritanical compromise: The giving up of cosmopolitan pleasures for work, for middle-class stability, for a voice that, in a smaller community, can be heard.

In Rochester Jerry and I have done our finest work. We have grown steadily in our professional careers and for that I am profoundly grateful.

As a woman I have grown in ways that are both exciting and unsettling. I have struggled to develop a life, a voice, a career that is apart from my husband's. This move that I dreaded has freed and forever altered me from a state of dependency. Had I not left New York, I might never have been forced to dredge up the resources that were within me. On the simplest levels I can drive a car, I can write, I can cope with three-foot snowdrifts in April, and a broken furnace in December. On a deeper level I know now I can survive alone, that I possess a rich inner life and the courage to follow its needs.

I am not at home. Perhaps I will never be "at home" again in that unselfconscious, uncritical way I once was. That is for the best. When I lived in New York I never wanted to budge.

I was chained to that town. For all my international background, I was the purest provincial New Yorker I have ever met.

I have now experienced, however reluctantly, pleasures that lie beyond the urban life. I have grown passionately attached to my vegetable garden—not to my house, not to Rochester—but to what used to be known as the basics of life —the seasonal tugs, the almost biological frenzy to plant on the first warm day of spring, supportive friends, bicycle riding at dusk when all those people who cannot stroll down Broadway or Madison Avenue are, instead, pruning their peonies or practicing guitar chords on their front porch.

Many of my New York friends grew up amid that normalcy and fled it. Well, for me it is a discovery, and although I have no illusion that my children, when they reach the threshold of adulthood, will find it exciting, for me it represents growth.

My office, on the third floor of our house, overlooks a hawthorn tree. In fall it is laden with clusters of fermenting berries upon which flocks of cedar waxwings get soused. Squirrels perform their high-wire acrobatics before me. In winter, cardinals flash by my window like ruby jets. To someone who works in monklike seclusion, such pleasures cannot make up for the choice of New York's distractions when the need to break out, to rejuice the mind and body takes over. My fantasy of the future is to have both: to commute between both worlds, to keep both my vegetable and mental gardens flourishing.

Looking back it is easy enough to see the stages one has passed through, to delude oneself into believing that the balance between pleasure and pain, between independence and mutuality, between growth and stability has finally been achieved. In my life, that is no longer true. I have no illusions anymore of safety, of permanence. I no longer see marriage as my permanent cocoon. Perhaps for me it has been a chrysalis from which some new and different creature will emerge.

One summer morning my husband looked up at me over a cup of coffee and said, with surprise and affection, "Well, we seem to be liking each other again. We seem to be happy."

I automatically replied, "I wonder how long that will last?"

We both laughed like crazy.